# AN EVEN BETTER PLACE

## America
## in the 21st Century

# RICHARD GEPHARDT

### WITH MICHAEL WESSEL

## PublicAffairs
### NEW YORK

Published in the United States by PublicAffairs™, a member of the Perseus Books Group.

Printed in the United States of America.

Book design by Jenny Dossin.

Library of Congress Cataloging-in-Publication Data

Gephardt, Richard A. (Richard Andrew), 1941-

An even better place : America in the 21st century / Richard Gephardt, with Michael Wessel.

p. cm.

ISBN 1–891620–16–9 (hc)

1. Management—Employee participation—United States. 2. United States—Economic policy—1993- —Citizen participation. 3. Economic forecasting—United States. 4. Family—United States. 5. Citizenship—United States. 6. Democracy—United States.

I. Wessel, Michael. II. Title.

HD5660.G47 1999

306'.0973—dc21 99–22339

CIP

10  9  8  7  6  5  4  3  2

To my parents,

FOR THE LIFE AND VALUES THEY GAVE ME.

To my wife, Jane,

FOR HER FRIENDSHIP AND LOVE.

And to my children, Matt, Chrissy, and Kate,

WHO DESERVE AN EVEN BETTER PLACE.

# CONTENTS

INTRODUCTION

# Democracy at Risk

# On the Brink of the Abyss

December 19, 1998, was a strange day. Although it was the Saturday before Christmas, it was sunny and warm in Washington, D.C., with temperatures rising into the sixties. The atmosphere inside the Capitol was even stranger. One day earlier, the House of Representatives had started debate on two articles of impeachment returned against President William Jefferson Clinton by the Republican majority in the House Judiciary Committee. Today, after another round of debate, those articles would come to a vote.

All of us understood the historic nature of the events unfolding in Congress. There had not been a debate and a vote like this on the floor of the House since the impeachment of President Andrew Johnson by the so-called Radical Republicans in 1868. For only the second time in our nation's 222-year history, we were about to put a sitting president on trial in the Senate. But there was an air of unreality to what we were doing; as if in some weird trance where the body behaves independently of the brain, we were helplessly enacting a drama that most of us dreaded and dearly wished to avoid.

My political instincts, honed by twenty-two years' experience in reading the mood of Congress, told me clearly that a majority of the House, including both Democrats and Republicans, preferred another outcome—a vote to harshly censure the president for carrying on a sexual affair with a White House intern and then misleading the public about it. It would have put the Congress on record as condemning the president's misdeeds while avoiding a drawn-out, sordid battle in the Senate and freeing both the executive and legislative branches to return to the people's business. Public opinion polls showed that most citizens preferred censure, too.

Yet it appeared that we wouldn't even have a chance to consider that option. The leadership of the Republican majority in the House was hell-bent on impeachment. They'd made it clear they would never let us vote on censure—precisely because they knew it might pass.

As the Minority Leader in the House, I was deeply frustrated by the unfairness of their decision. As I'd come to know firsthand during the previous four years, members of the minority party in Congress often think the procedures dictated by the majority are unfair. But on almost all issues, the majority generally allows the minority the chance to propose and vote on an alternative they prefer. It's a matter of political etiquette and common respect among public servants who, after all, must find ways to work together for the good of the nation.

And today's was no ordinary issue. We were deciding whether to launch the process that could lead to the overturning of a national election for the first time in American history. (Even Andrew Johnson's impeachment was no precedent in this respect; Johnson was never elected president but took office after the assassination of Lincoln.) Nonetheless, the Republicans were adamant: No alternative to impeachment could be considered. They even declared it a matter, not of politics, but of "conscience."

4

Apparently those who favored impeachment would get a chance to vote their consciences, but the rest of us wouldn't.

That strange December morning, with the second day of the impeachment debate already under way, I was sitting at my desk in my office in the Capitol, writing what would be my second speech in two days on impeachment. At home the night before, I had pulled from my bookshelf John F. Kennedy's classic political history, *Profiles in Courage.* I reread his account of the heroism of Senator Edmund G. Ross of Kansas, one of seven Republicans who broke with their party to vote against the impeachment of Andrew Johnson. In so doing, Ross destroyed his own political career—he and the others were drummed out of office by bitter fellow party members—but he may well have preserved the balance of powers so artfully established in our nation's Constitution. His was truly a vote of conscience.

In the speech I was drafting that morning, I quoted Ross's famous comment about how he'd felt as he prepared to cast the fateful, deciding vote: "I almost literally looked down into my open grave. Friendships, position, fortune, everything that makes life desirable to an ambitious man were about to be swept away by the breath of my mouth, perhaps forever." Yet in the face of overwhelming partisan pressure Ross stood firm, casting his vote for what he believed was right. Even at the eleventh hour I was hoping against hope that his moving story might somehow shame the House leadership into allowing us, after all, our own vote of conscience.

As I scribbled away at my desk, I glanced from time to time at the television set a few feet away, tuned as usual to C-SPAN. Bob Livingston of Louisiana was addressing the House of Representatives. He was the man we all knew was going to be elected Speaker of the House in January, replacing the controversial Newt Gingrich, who'd startled Washington by resigning suddenly after Republican losses in the midterm elections just two months before. Now Livingston himself was at the center of controversy: Just two days before, in anticipation of an about-to-break news story, he'd appeared before his Republican colleagues to confess having had more than one adulterous affair. He'd asked their forgiveness and support, and they'd responded with a standing ovation.

As I wrote, I listened with half an ear to the low murmur of Livingston's comments on the TV. Suddenly, my press secretary, Laura Nichols, rushed into the room. She said, "There's a rumor on the floor that Livingston is going to resign!" She turned up the volume, and others on my staff joined me around the set to listen to Livingston's speech.

For a few moments, at least, his remarks were unsurprising, as he methodically laid out the Republican rationale for impeachment. Then, unexpectedly, he called on President Clinton to end the impeachment ordeal—by resigning. Frustrated and angry, a few Democrats shouted catcalls from the floor: "*You* should quit instead!" "Resign! Resign!"

To the shock of everyone listening, he did. "I was prepared to lead our narrow majority as Speaker," Livingston said. "And I believe I had it in me to do a fine job. But I cannot do that job or be the kind of leader that I would like to be under the current circumstances. So I must set the example that I hope President Clinton will follow. I will not stand for Speaker of the House on January 6."

I was dumbfounded. Bob Livingston had come to Congress a few years after me. My wife Jane and I had known Bob and his wife, Bonnie, for many years, and I really liked him. We didn't agree on many policy matters, but I'd always felt he was fair, respected his adversaries, and respected the institution of the House of Representatives. Now, this decent, widely admired public servant was suddenly gone.

For me, this was the last straw. In my recent speeches, I'd been decrying what I called the politics of personal destruction: the assassination of public reputations by innuendo, gossip, accusation, and leak. An out-of-control special prosecutor and a right-wing rumor mill had singled out the president as their target. Now the Speaker-designate had been dragged down, victimized by a newspaper story inspired by pornographer Larry Flynt's gleeful probing into Republicans' sex lives. And there was no end in sight.

This was no brand-new phenomenon. In retrospect, we'd been in an accelerating downward spiral of political and personal destruction for some twenty-five years. I'd seen a lot of it up close. I hated it. And now, as the cycle of attack and retribution grew even fiercer, I felt frightened for our country that I love so much. I could almost see the fabric of mutual respect that holds together our fragile experiment in self-governance unraveling before my eyes.

As the televised scene on C-SPAN broke into a new uproar, I tossed aside the papers on which I'd been scribbling. "Laura," I said, "I can't give this speech. I've got to write a new one." Just then, Congressman Joe Kennedy, a good friend of mine, burst into the office, almost breathless in his haste. "Did you hear? Livingston just resigned! The floor is a mess—you've got to get out there. Our members are booing him—you've got to quiet them down!"

I told Joe I'd be out as soon as I could. In a moment, David Bonior, the Democratic Whip, rushed in with virtually the same message. I asked him to try to calm the troops, and I promised again that I'd be out as soon as I could. The next thing I knew, C-SPAN was broadcasting the voice of John Conyers, ranking Democrat on the Judiciary Committee, announcing me on the floor as the next Democratic speaker.

"Dan!" I yelled to one of our staffers who handles the floor of the House. "Run out to the floor and tell John that I'm not ready— I'll come as soon as I can." The C-SPAN screen was now blank. Viewers around the nation had been told that Dick Gephardt was the next speaker on impeachment—but that no one knew where he was.

I was livid. The president was being impeached. The Republican leader had resigned. And the Democratic leader had been announced but couldn't be found. People everywhere must have been thinking, *What kind of madness is ruling Washington?*

Taking a deep breath, I sat back down at my desk and talked with Laura and Eric London, my speechwriter, about what I wanted to say. We scribbled down our thoughts, and Eric and Laura ran out to type them up. A few minutes later, they came back with a single sheet. I scanned it quickly and realized that I didn't like the ending. The first speech I'd been writing—the one I'd just torn up—ended with a prayer. God knew we needed that more now than ever. I grabbed the typed speech, wrote a prayer in longhand, and headed toward the floor.

I'd taken that same walk to the floor of the House—that grand, exhilarating, exasperating, *human* institution I truly love—countless times before, but rarely with such an intense mix of emotions. My throat was dry and I was nervous, but the message I had to deliver was one I felt very deeply. From experience, I knew this meant I could say it and get it across.

When I reached the lectern in the well of the House, I could feel tension—even fear—in the room. I delivered my speech:

I stood on the floor of the House yesterday and implored you: The politics of slash and burn must end.

I implored all of you that we must turn away from the politics of personal destruction and return to a politics of values.

It is with that same passion that I say today that Bob Livingston is a worthy and honorable man. And that his decision to retire is a terrible capitulation to the negative forces that are consuming our political system and our country.

I pray with all my heart that he will reconsider his decision.

Our founding fathers created a system of government of men, not of angels. No one standing in this House today can pass a puritanical test of purity that some are demanding that our elected leaders take.

If we demand that mere mortals live up to this standard, we will see our seats of government lay empty, and we will see the best, most able people unfairly cast out of public service.

We need to stop destroying imperfect people at the altar of an unattainable morality. We need to start living up to the standards which the public, in its wisdom, understands that imperfect people must strive for, though too often we fall short.

We are now rapidly descending into a politics where life imitates farce, fratricide dominates our public debate, and America is held hostage to tactics of smear and fear.

Let all of us here say no to resignation, no to impeachment, no to hatred, no intolerance of each other, and no to vicious self-righteousness.

We need to start healing. We need to end this downward spiral which will culminate in the death of representative democracy.

I believe this healing can start today by changing the course we've begun. This is exactly why we need today to be bipartisan.

This is why we ask for the opportunity to vote on a bipartisan censure resolution—to begin the process of healing our nation and healing our people.

We are on the brink of the abyss. The only way we stop this insanity is through the force of our own will—for all of us to simply say "enough." Let's step back from the abyss. And let's begin a new politics of respect and decency and fairness which rises above what has come before.

May God have mercy on this Congress. And may Congress have the wisdom and the courage to save itself today.

As I walked up the aisle after my speech, several members grabbed and hugged me. Many of us had tears in our eyes. What was in my heart was in their hearts. We all knew something terrible was happening to us. We all wanted the destruction to end. But none of us knew how to do it. We all knew it wouldn't be easy.

In the days since that speech, hundreds of citizens have come up to me—on the street, in airports, in restaurants—to thank me for my words. "You said what I feel" is the common message. In thirty years of public service, I never before received such a reaction. Americans are so decent and good. They want us to do better. They want the politics of destruction to end. When will we summon the will to stop it?

## The Roots of Political Destruction

Politics, I like to say, is a substitute for violence. From our roots as warring tribes and factions, we've risen by many slow and painful steps. We've learned to talk through our differences, to submit to judgment by laws and juries, to make decisions collectively, to choose and follow leaders. Each advance toward self-governance has reduced our reliance on force as a means of resolving disagreements. In this sense, politics is not only a noble calling, but also perhaps our only real alternative to chaos.

It's easy for us to fall back from civil society into violence. The persistence of warfare between nations is one example, of course. But so is our tendency—during times of heightened emotion, competition, and stress—to revert to violence and near-violence in our social and political lives, figuratively killing one another through personal assaults upon one another's character, integrity, and humanity.

We deplore this, of course, but our dirty little secret is that it comes so naturally to us as human beings to attack, to smear, to assassinate. The lust to retaliate with lethal force is understandable, but the cycle of violence and political destruction thus begun has no natural ending.

When our political life is caught up in such a cycle, we gradually destroy our belief in ourselves and our democracy. We cause our citizens to hate their leaders and their government, to become cynical, apathetic, and indifferent. In time, they drop out and begin treating politics as just another form of gladiatorial entertainment; they start electing professional wrestlers as governors.

I suspect the cycle we're in today started with the Watergate scandal. The constitutional issues raised by President Richard Nixon's unethical behavior were serious and may even have warranted impeachment. Perhaps inevitably, however, the process itself was a bloody mess, resulting in the destruction of dozens of reputations and lasting animus between the two major political parties.

Technically, Nixon was not impeached; he resigned the presidency after the House Judiciary Committee voted to approve articles of impeachment but before the matter reached the House floor. However, the effect was the same. The most radical act provided for in the Constitution—the overturning of a national election—occurred. A lot of people who disagreed with the result were furious; some of them still are.

Since the time of Watergate, we've careened from personal attack to counterattack right up through the impeachment of Bill Clinton. Supreme Court nominees have been knocked out in pitched battles that, in retrospect, look like target practice. We had the so-called Debategate during the Carter administration, the Iran-Contra affair during the Reagan administration, and the October Surprise and the draft-record scandal during the Bush administration. New heights—or depths—have been reached during the Clinton administration: In fact, the attack machine was turned on during Bill Clinton's first presidential campaign ("draft dodger," "didn't inhale") and has never been turned off.

## The Death of Citizenship?

Most disturbing is that the cycle of destruction in our politics is slowly but surely turning citizens away from participating in self-government. The demise of our democracy may be the final result.

I have a Russian friend, Grigory Yavlinsky, who leads a reform-minded party in the Duma, or the Russian legislature. A few months back, I asked Grigory what he thought was the greatest problem in his troubled, struggling homeland. He thought for a while and then said, "Here is the trouble with Russia: If you need chess players, we've got them. If you need nuclear physicists, we're loaded. If you need ballet dancers, we have the best. But if you need *citizens*, we don't have any."

Grigory explained, "For centuries, we had czars; then we had communism. Either way, we were always told what to think and what to do. Now we are trying to reach for capitalism and democracy, and we don't know how to do it. Our people don't know how to form parties, how to develop agendas, or how to run for office." He concluded, "Until we become thinking, independent, participating citizens, we will not have either democracy or capitalism."

Isn't it ironic? Just as Russia, South Korea, South Africa, and many other countries around the world are seeking to emulate our centuries-old experiment in democracy, our own citizens are becoming cynical, embittered, and apathetic toward it. They are increasingly uninterested in the arts of citizenship my friend Grigory so rightly admires.

And participation in American elections is getting worse and worse. In a 1998 primary election in my home state of Missouri, the voter turnout was less than *15 percent*! Too many people don't bother to register to vote; more and more don't want to identify with any political party or candidate. In polls and surveys, people are quick to agree that the system is corrupt and that everyone in government is selfish, crooked, and craven.

On the Sunday morning talk shows, politicians and pundits bemoan this state of affairs. But why are we surprised by it? Isn't it natural that our citizens, after a quarter-century of the politics of personal destruction, are left with the impression that everybody in politics is bad and that the whole system is corrupt? No wonder millions of people are in retreat from the idea of taking part in the rites and privileges of citizenship.

This steady erosion of the concept of citizenship is having other dangerous effects. The politics of personal destruction discourages citizens from running for office or accepting government appointments. It has always been difficult to get talented people to forgo private employment in favor of the generally lower pay and more modest perks of public service. Now add the excruciating examination of every aspect of their lives and you can see why fewer and fewer people are willing to even consider public office. If this continues, the only people available for government service will be talentless nonentities who've never said or done anything controversial or interesting in their lives.

Second, the politics of personal destruction is gradually destroying the ability of legislative bodies to perform their critical role of resolving society's important conflicts. If there is no trust or civility among members of Congress, there is little ability to address our nation's major challenges.

When I came to Congress in the late 1970s, the debates were fierce but the friendships—even between members in different political parties—were strong. The politics of destruction were not yet in full swing and people could still find ways to effectively compromise their views without giving up their heartfelt values. House members could disagree without being disagreeable. When Tom Foley, the last Democratic Speaker, rose to disagree with a colleague, he always started his comments with the words "with respect." These weren't empty words. He wasn't just saying those words to say them. He really did respect his adversaries as people even though he disagreed with them on issues. His statement of respect let his adversary know his disagreement did not imply personal dislike. I once explained how this must be done by comparing it to marriage. I've been married to Jane Gephardt for thirty-two years and we've often disagreed on many things. But we never lost our underlying love and respect for one another.

Dick Bolling, a highly partisan Democratic member of the House from Missouri and my mentor in Congress, once told me, "Nothing big and important for the country was ever passed here that wasn't bipartisan." Dick was right. Significant problems can usually be solved only in a bipartisan manner, which requires the members to compromise and give up some of their political advantage in the interests of a greater good. That cannot happen when partisan warfare is under way.

## Ending the Madness

We can bring an end to the politics of personal destruction only when enough people, in politics and in every walk of life, insist upon it. In Ireland, after generations of sectarian warfare, more and more citizens have come to see the futility of violence as a means of settling disputes. Today there is finally a critical mass of Irish citizens, Protestant and Catholic alike, who want peace and are willing to take moral and political risks to achieve it. And as a direct result, there is now peace—an uneasy peace, but peace nonetheless. This same kind of change of heart is essential for American politics.

We must start by getting political leaders on both sides of the aisle to understand and acknowledge just what it is we have been doing to ourselves and our country. So many politicians have been dragged into the cycle of destruction that they are not even fully aware of what is happening. Inflamed by partisan passions, angry from the assaults they and their friends have suffered, they say that the only way to handle attacks is to counterattack. (Of course, to do so simply perpetuates the cycle of destruction.) It's time to face up to that reality and say, "No more."

In addition, we must consciously foster a rebirth of civic activism and mutual tolerance and respect among all of our citizens. Ultimately, it's up to every man and woman in the nation to sustain our democracy. To do this, we must reassume the full mantle of *citizenship*—as active participants, supporters, reformers, and creators, not just of our government but of all our institutions—of our neighborhoods, of our schools, of our health system, and of our businesses.

The passive role of spectator-consumer is no longer enough. The current mess in Washington shows what can happen when average Americans stop voting, stop participating, and let politicians treat government as their own private power game. It's our government, it's our country, and it's time we took them both back.

It is true that I have been labeled a liberal, which for many suggests an image of big, intrusive government with a program for every problem. But to me, the foundation of liberalism is community activism and citizen participation. That's the path I followed in my rise to political office. All Americans must learn again to think like owners about national institutions—owners who demand the power to shape their own lives and who accept the responsibilities that go along with that power.

I started to write this book before the impeachment of President Clinton and my speech on the floor of the House of Representatives about the politics of destruction. I've been thinking about writing this book for a long time—to be exact, since 1988, when I ran for president. As that race brought home to me, a politician today gets few chances to explain his views in any depth; the microphones, the cameras, the public mind all move on quickly. Today's media favors 5-second sound bites and sticking everyone in a "pigeonhole" for quick and easy identification. But some ideas and some issues demand a more thoughtful discussion than mere sound bites permit. That's why writing a book appealed to me.

After thirty years in public life, I'm hardly a stranger—certainly not to my constituents in Missouri or my colleagues in the Congress. But this book is the first opportunity I've had to speak in depth about the major challenges we Americans face, and it's the first time I've described my personal background to help explain the sources of my views.

During the decade since I first considered writing a book, I've found that some of my positions have changed, occasionally in ways that surprised me. I like to think I've grown as a politician; as you'll learn in these pages, I've had to acknowledge more than once having been on the wrong side of a particular issue. In other cases, I think my positions have been further buttressed by recent events. All in all, this is a very different book than the one I might have written ten years ago—in part because we live in very different times.

I also realized last December during the impeachment process that the resulting loss of interest in participating in politics and civic life by our citizens, and what we can do about it, was the common theme that threads through this entire book and the ideas expressed in it. In the 1988 campaign and since, I have realized that, as much as I believe government has an important and vital role in meeting our present challenges, I also believe that we will never meet these challenges without a renewal of citizen participation in reasserting our ownership over civic and private institutions and our country itself. We must replace the politics of destruction with a new politics of values, ideals, and participation.

American democracy is seriously threatened. The trouble begins in Washington, where the degree of partisan animosity is greater than I've ever seen. At one time, Democrats and Republicans might fight hard for their differing convictions on the floor of the House, then go out afterward for a friendly beer together, like rivals in a neighborhood softball league. Those days seem to be gone. Now, Democrats and Republicans don't even make eye contact when they pass one another in the halls of Congress, unless it's to exchange furious glares. That's how deep the hostility engendered by years of personal attacks has gone. And the personal animosity leads to intransigence, mud-slinging, and political vendettas, while the work of the people is neglected.

Even worse, the problem today extends far beyond Washington. The same hostile, partisan atmosphere we see in Washington is seen in state legislatures and city councils all over America. The incivility we see among leaders is being emulated by many other citizens. Partly as a reaction to the partisan dogfighting they see on their nightly news, Americans everywhere have been turning away from politics, not bothering to vote, not bothering to hope. The result, of course, is a vicious cycle, because as fewer people vote, the influence of those at the extremes—who do vote—becomes ever greater.

But Americans have reason to hope and reason to vote, and in this book I'll try to show why. This isn't a book about the legislation I've passed or about the famous people on both sides of the aisle I've worked with—and done battle with—although I'll talk a little about such matters. Nor is it a book about how nice a fellow

I am, although you'll inevitably get to know a bit more about me as I describe some of the events and people that have influenced my thinking. It's both a self-help guide to the challenges we Americans face in the new world economy and a message of concern— and ultimately optimism—about the state of citizen involvement in our democracy. Most of all, it's a call to action.

That's why I've chosen to write this book now: because we live in a time of testing for our country, and I hope my voice can make a difference. Today, I think, is our chance—perhaps our last, best chance—to get back on the right track. We can do it only by re-claiming ownership of the land we love.

Sadly, impeachment and the politics of personal destruction have become the window through which the public views politi-cians and public policy. Over the past year, as the cycle of destruc-tion has reached its nadir, the public has increasingly questioned why political leaders insist on engaging in partisan skirmishing while doing little to address our nation's problems, and health care coverage, economic equity, retirement and job security, and many other needs continue to go unmet. It's no wonder that average, hardworking Americans feel alienated from Washington.

Both our political leaders and the public must act, because the challenges we face can't be solved by government or by private citizens alone. Political leaders must lead by example and individ-uals must renew their citizenship.

Public leaders must continue to fight for what they believe; there are deep differences between the parties on important pol-icy issues, and our views and values are worth defending. But we must make the issues our battleground and seek resolution—not simply pursue conflict for the sake of political gain.

And government alone won't solve the problems our country

faces. We need to reinvigorate our sense of citizenship by encouraging all Americans to participate more actively in promoting the changes needed to reclaim control of our national destiny. In part, this is a book about how all citizens can play their part—through greater awareness and involvement in the political process, yes, but also by working to build more responsive and effective school systems, to make our workplaces more productive, democratic, and fair, and to ensure that every family has access to basic health care and a social safety net in times of need. It's understandable that the dismaying spectacle presented by Washington politics too often in recent years has turned off millions of our citizens. But that's an attitude we just can't afford any longer.

I've written this book to try to explain why reclaiming this sense of ownership is crucial to our future, and also to share the stories of citizens I've met from every walk of life who are doing just that. I hope you'll find these stories as inspiring as I do.

Even more important, I hope you'll use this book as a guide to how all Americans can take back ownership of our schools, our businesses, our communities, and, ultimately, our shared political life. I believe that if enough of us respond, America in the twenty-first century, reformed and enriched by the unique contributions of every citizen, can become for all of us an even better place.

# I
# Thinking
# Like Owners

DEMOCRACY IN THE WORKPLACE

AND THE MARKETPLACE

# "We're All in This Together"

I suppose most people are deeply influenced by their childhood experiences. I'm no exception. I grew up in St. Louis during the 1940s and 1950s, as part of a working-class family very much in the economic mainstream for the time. My attitudes and beliefs about work, family, community, and basic fairness are still shaped by my memories of those years.

We baby boomers sometimes look back on those postwar days through a haze of nostalgia, as if they were a golden era of prosperity and happiness. But like most rose-colored memories, that's at best a half-truth. I remember how my family struggled financially. Almost all of the clothes I wore as a child were hand-me-downs from relatives who were better off than we were. We had a beat-up used car, a 1937 Ford two-door, that Dad constantly worked on to keep it going. But our primary mode of transportation was the public bus and streetcar system in St. Louis. We took the bus everywhere. I remember many days and nights standing out in harsh cold or oppressive heat, waiting forty-five minutes, sometimes an hour, for a bus to come.

My dad set a family pattern of frugality. He always used to say that the only way to have money was to not spend it. All during my childhood, Dad kept a big garden and canned the vegetables he grew there for our family to eat. Growing up, he'd been deeply affected by the Depression and always talked about how the only way his family had survived those hard times was by feeding themselves from their garden.

When I was little, Dad supported our family by driving a milk truck. He didn't make a lot of money, but he always told us that he would have been paid a lot less if he hadn't been a member of the Teamsters Union. He often talked disparagingly about the "big shots," about how people with wealth took advantage of the "little guy." The union, he felt, was the worker's best friend and ally.

Dad wasn't bitter about the occasional harshness of life. There was a sense that this was just the way things were. Anyway, he wasn't the only one working hard. Everyone pitched in. My mom worked as a secretary, and my brother Don and I usually worked weekends and summers. Life was similar for other families in the neighborhood. Everyone we knew took it for granted that you worked hard and shared rewards as a family and as a community. I can never thank my parents enough for the sacrifices and struggles they made for me. My views on work and unions and the struggles of working families were shaped in this period. From these experiences I knew I wanted to someday help families like mine. I never will forget where I came from and how much my family meant to me.

So I was raised to believe in the dignity of work, even though we didn't always talk about it in that way. I now understand that it's a central value to the American way as well as to my Baptist tradition and my wife Jane's Catholic faith. Like most Americans, I believe that there's an inherent value in all people's efforts to do something useful to support themselves and their families. And although times were sometimes tough in postwar America, there was a concrete commitment to the idea that work was to be honored and rewarded. Throughout the 1940s and 1950s, wages were rising. People in our neighborhood were always buying new things—their first car, TV set, or washing machine—things we take for granted today but that were luxuries for the time. Our bit of the American dream included our family's first house. Dad bought it in 1942 for $4,000 and made only interest payments on it. He eventually sold it in 1965 for all of $13,000—a pretty good return on his investment, we all agreed.

As the postwar recovery turned into a great economic boom, average American families in St. Louis and around the country had the feeling that all of us would share some of the benefits. What made that possible? There's no single answer. Dad was right about the role of strong labor unions—they certainly played a part. So did government guarantees, such as the minimum wage, workers' compensation, and Social Security. But an unspoken ethic of respect for the worker largely permeated corporate America as well. Even as a kid, I understood that the big St. Louis companies like Anheuser-Busch, Monsanto, and McDonnell-Douglas generally treated their employees with decency and fairness. It was a world in which aerospace workers and electricians, steelworkers and stenographers, truck drivers and teachers could all hold their heads high, a world where kids were proud of their parents. Many hoped to follow in their parents' footsteps—in fact, many parents helped their kids get a job at their workplace and then worked side-by-side with them, in a genuine family atmosphere.

If people today consider the 1950s the good old days, then I think it's because of a shared belief that we were in it together—that other families in our neighborhood faced the same problems and enjoyed the same opportunities we did. We shared in the successes and supported one another throughout the failures. I remember how the whole neighborhood turned out when the first car arrived outside someone's house. There was pride in what they had accomplished, and little jealousy, because we sensed that in time and with hard work all Americans could achieve the good life.

## The Devaluing of Work

Today, in too many ways, work and working people are being devalued. Many have come to feel that the good life comes only to a fortunate few—those who inherit a family fortune or those blessed with exceptional talent in business, entertainment, or sports. Hard work at an everyday job looks like a sucker's bet to many of our youth. Though we've nominally increased the minimum wage, its actual value has eroded to the point where many of the working poor would do better on welfare. In the words of Raul Yzaguirre, president of La Raza, America's largest grassroots Hispanic organization, some must make the terrible choice "between their children and their pride." And blue-collar and white-collar Americans, with relatively few exceptions, have seen their earning power stagnate, despite steady increases in the length and productivity of their working hours.

Furthermore, many Americans have become ambivalent in their attitudes toward work itself. Shortly after I was first elected to serve in Congress, I began what I called "work days"—days spent back home in St. Louis, doing different jobs. I was a garbage collector for a day and a bagger at a grocery store; I rode around town in an ambulance, working with emergency medical technicians.

My campaign staff saw these days as opportunities for the people of my district to relate to me person-to-person, as an ordinary

Joe, rather than on a pedestal as their congressman. (We midwesterners don't appreciate it when anyone gets a little too big for their britches.) But for me it was a chance to learn from the people I worked with and met. Hanging on to the handrails of a garbage truck you quickly learn that people ignore or avoid trash collectors. To them, it's an undignified occupation most people don't want their kids to follow. Only when the sanitation workers go out on strike does the public fully realize how vital a role they play.

Still, despite the fact that they didn't have glamorous jobs, the sanitation workers I rode with were quietly proud of their work. They weren't getting rich, but they were getting by, thanks to their own efforts. I worked with a man who'd been collecting trash for the city for twenty-five years. He taught me how to lift the heavy trash cans properly, throw the contents into the truck, and toss the cans back onto the street—there's a craft and a technique to this work as there is to everything. As we drove around town, he told me about his four kids. "I don't have a great job," he remarked, "but I sure am proud of the education my children got. They'll never have to throw garbage like I did." Two of his children were lawyers, and two were doctors. His story speaks volumes about the importance and dignity of work.

Working women everywhere share these feelings. Some time ago, I asked Karen Nussbaum, who headed up 9-to-5, the organization representing workingwomen, to set up sessions for me with workingwomen in different cities. One woman in Boston spoke for millions: "I've got a job. I go out in the morning to work. I want my children to see that."

Every working person seeks and deserves respect for his or her efforts. Yet today there is a growing divide between people who work with their hands and so-called knowledge workers, the well-educated elite who are the vanguard of the information age. Clearly, the advent of new technology is revolutionizing the world and creating remarkable new career opportunities. But the fact is that there are countless jobs that need to be done that are neither glamorous nor stepping-stones to a better job. The increasing gulf between "good" jobs and "bad" jobs has demeaned the dignity of too many people. Every job should be considered a good job if you work hard and play by the rules, and all who work deserve our respect and our thanks. They don't always get them.

In 1988, I campaigned for the presidential nomination. Traveling the country, I met many workers who barely earned enough to get by, although they worked hard every day. Their courage and fortitude impressed me deeply. I remember the workers from a paper plant in Jay, Maine, who'd been on strike for more than six months. Many were working odd jobs, doing whatever they could to stay out of bankruptcy. Although they'd seen their regular jobs taken by scab workers—nonunion replacements—they refused to back down or cross the picket lines; that's how determined they were to keep faith with the union and their fellow workers.

In Boston I met a young man working as a mental-health aide in a hospital who expressed the emotions of many in today's less-prestigious occupations: "We always feel like we're the leftovers." It's a feeling the working-class people of St. Louis rarely felt back in the 1950s, and as a nation we need to address its social and economic causes.

Today the United States is experiencing its eighth straight year of economic growth. This should be unalloyed good news. Yet many families don't feel they're fully sharing in the benefits of that growth, and even economists are uncertain about what's really happening. For example, the president's Council of Economic Advisers claims that most of the new jobs being created in the current expansion are "good" jobs, defined as jobs in industries that pay above-average wages. Yet in many cases the new job at a fast-growing high-tech company may in fact be a low-paying secretarial, janitorial, or clerical position rather than a well-paying plum for a software programmer. Is that really a "good" job? You decide.

In 1996, former Senator Bob Dole pointed out during his second debate with President Clinton that the biggest employer in America today is not General Motors, Microsoft, or Wal-Mart; it's Manpower Services, a temporary employment agency: "Hiring people temporarily who've lost their jobs and they go to work for 30 days or 60 days. That's a good economy? I don't think so." Unfortunately, evidence from around the country largely supports Dole's view. For example, in Louisville, Kentucky, the largest source of new jobs is United Parcel Service (UPS), whose brown delivery trucks are familiar everywhere. The company has a large regional distribution center in town. The trouble is that a substantial portion of the more than 14,000 jobs at UPS are now part-time positions. Part-time jobs generally pay lower wages. The workers often have no real chance of advancement—rather, they're at higher risk for layoffs whenever the economy suffers a downturn. Part-time jobs also rarely offer any kind of health or pension benefits, increasing the financial and health insecurity of employees and their families.

# Two Sides of the Knowledge Economy

In the expanding postwar St. Louis of my youth, manufacturing drove the economy's growth. Eager to enjoy all the new consumer goods of the day, Americans were buying cars, appliances, TVs, furniture, you name it—and millions of jobs were created to satisfy the demand. Today, that's changed. Since 1979 America has lost more than 2.5 million manufacturing jobs—many of them the kind of good-paying jobs that used to lift Americans up and into the middle class. Today, only about one employee in seven is in the manufacturing sector.

Of course, the diversity of new jobs being created is astounding. Many are found in industries that didn't exist a short time ago—software, fiber optics, biotechnology. Many are the kinds of high-skill, high-salary jobs we'd want for ourselves and our children. We need to aggressively promote jobs in these industries, expanding the so-called knowledge-based economy to include as many people as possible.

My own family is a good illustration of how the service sector—in particular the knowledge economy—is playing a more and more dominant role in our future.

Like all our kids, our son, Matt, graduated from public grade school and high school in Virginia. After high school, he applied to several universities, and we visited colleges around the country. We wanted Matt to realize that he could go anywhere he wanted to go. All I could think was that if my milk truck–driving Dad could help me go to Northwestern University I should be able to help my kids pursue their dreams almost anywhere.

When Matt was accepted into Duke University he was thrilled, and his four years there were terrific. Later, I encouraged Matt to consider law school, which I'd found to be such great training. But he ultimately focused on business school, attending his parents' alma mater, Northwestern.

Matt especially loved his class in entrepreneurship, where he and two of his classmates put together a business plan that their professor thought was terrific. I won't give away any secrets, but the idea is a new one in the sports-marketing field. Since graduating, the three of them have formed a corporation to try to bring their idea to fruition. Who knows? Maybe they'll match the achievements of Federal Express founder Fred Smith, who created a new business—and a whole new industry—based on an idea he developed as a student in business school.

Our middle child, Chrissy, followed in my footsteps, attending the Junior High School Institute at Northwestern and ultimately attending the Speech School there. Today, Chrissy is a manager at Southwestern Bell in St. Louis. She loves working with people and is putting all of her speech and group dynamics training to work on the job every day. We're very proud of her accomplishments. Her husband, Marc Leibole, a classmate of hers at Northwestern, is in medical school at Washington University in St. Louis.

Kate, our youngest, is now finishing up at the School of Education at Vanderbilt University. Kate has always dreamed of being a teacher, and Jane and I have done everything we could to encourage her. After graduation (May 1999), Kate wants to study early childhood education in graduate school. She's lucky enough to really love children; she enjoys nothing more than teaching them and watching them develop, and I think she has a wonderful future to look forward to.

Matt, Chrissy, and Kate—a budding entrepreneur, a manager in a telecommunications business, a future educator—all have been able to turn the advantages of a secure upbringing and a fine education into promising careers. All three are pursuing the kind of work that offers the greatest potential rewards in the new economy—demanding and responsible, learning-intensive, and long on "people skills."

Unfortunately, not everyone is faring so well in the knowledge economy. Many of the newly created jobs in the service sector don't pay very well and, in many cases, provide no benefits—jobs ranging from flipping burgers and caring for our children and parents to clerking in a department store or adjusting insurance claims. As manufacturing jobs have declined, the jobs that have replaced them haven't always been the quality jobs that promote a high and rising standard of living.

The U.S. Department of Labor publishes an annual assessment of job growth. In its 1998–1999 edition, the department lists occupations that will create the most new jobs over the next ten years. Among the top-growing professions are cashiers, retail sales clerks, home-health aides, truck drivers, nurses aides, and receptionists.

Make no mistake: These are important jobs in our economy. These are the people who make sure that our children are nurtured, that fresh produce reaches our dinner tables, that our buildings are safe, and that our elderly parents are cared for, among many other tasks. Yet these jobs don't receive the respect accorded to financiers, attorneys, or physicians. And on the most basic, most important level, they don't always pay a living wage. *It's just not fair.*

The Catholic Church has spoken out countless times on this issue. In their 1986 pastoral letter, America's Catholic bishops put it eloquently: "We have many partial ways to measure and debate the health of our economy—gross national product, per capita income, stock market prices. The Christian vision of economic life looks beyond them all and asks, Does economic life enhance or threaten our life together as a community?" For me, that's the crucial question.

Many of us feel that current trends in our economy are damaging rather than enhancing our life as a community. The statistics tell part of the story. Although our economy has been growing and unemployment is at historically low levels, not everyone is benefiting to the same degree. From 1989 to 1997, for example, the average income of the top 1 percent of families grew by 10 percent, whereas the income of people in the middle grew by only 0.2 percent and that of the people at the bottom grew by only 0.1 percent. In the years since then, the trend seems to have begun to change, but those at the top are still doing much better than everyone else. Hard work is simply no longer the ticket to a decent life that it used to be.

## Creeping Insecurity

Americans are an inherently optimistic people. Maybe it's a legacy of our frontier past, perhaps the natural result of the fact that we're a nation of immigrants—people who sought these shores in the belief that life could be better for themselves and their children. So I find it particularly disturbing that more and more Americans today feel insecure about their long-term futures. They don't always put it in personal terms. More often, they talk about their children, their neighbors, their communities. Many people feel they're doing all right—but they worry about whether the same will be true five years or ten years from now.

In the America of my youth, annual salary increases were the norm, made possible by the country's booming productivity and by the combined efforts of labor unions and a government that viewed itself as an ally of working people. No more. For most workers at all levels of the economic ladder wages were stagnant or even falling until very recently. And the minimal wage gains we've seen during the last few months have failed to make a dent in real incomes, which for most Americans have only recently begun to exceed 1979 levels.

To get ahead, people are taking on more jobs and longer hours. What they've been unable to achieve through raises they've made up for by being willing to work harder and harder. According to the Economic Policy Institute in Washington, D.C., between 1989 and 1996 the typical middle-class couple took on the equivalent of more than six weeks of extra work per year.

Businesses certainly benefit from their employees' longer workweeks. If an employer can simply load more hours on the existing workforce, it saves the cost of hiring a new employee; it won't have to pay for health benefits, training, insurance, and the like. At the same time, many employees *want* the overtime. Many, in fact, are scrambling for it. I once read a story of an autoworker who was working more than *eighty hours* per week in order to save for the future. His family income was approaching $100,000 a year, but he didn't want to let up. He didn't dare.

People today are willing to work extraordinarily hard because they're never sure when a downturn might hit. They want to do as well as they can for as long as they can. If that means more time on the job, so be it. Clearly, without rising wages and incomes, this is what families have to do to stay even, much less get ahead. But there are some real prices we all pay: increased stress for workers and their families; health risks; less time with spouses, friends, and children; less time for involvement in the community, schools, churches, and synagogues. Civil society suffers in an anxious, wage-driven world.

Time-stress affects working people in ways that are obvious and not so obvious. I met a woman who worked as a carpenter at a construction site. During her morning coffee break, she used to sneak away and rush home to drive her young daughter to school, praying she'd be able to get back to the job before the foreman noticed her absence. Talk about stress!

Even the phrase "lunch hour" seems to have become outdated. A survey reported in *Investor's Business Daily* found that the average lunch break is now thirty-six minutes. Most office workers say they have to do other things besides eating during lunch hour—and 40 percent use part of the time to catch up on work.

At the same time, people are increasingly connected to their workplaces by electronic leashes—pagers, cellular phones, home computers, faxes. For some, this increases their flexibility, but for others it means that they can never escape the pressures of their jobs. They're always on call. Again, all other aspects of life suffer.

Part of the reason for this is the fact that many businesses are now global. When it's nighttime here, it may be midday for a client in Japan, Australia, or Ukraine. And the pace of business is speeding up: Product-development cycles are being shortened, capital markets operate electronically around the clock, competition is intensifying.

But worker insecurity is increasing, too, and employees often feel they *must* be available around the clock because of competition for the jobs they hold. ("If I don't take that 2 A.M. call, they'll hire somebody who will.") Working people are reminded almost daily that practically everyone is now expendable. Amid a rising economy, few commentators have noticed that we have also seen the highest level of downsizings and layoffs ever. Layoffs in 1998 were more than 50 percent higher than the year before.

Until now, the economy has been able to absorb most of the laid-off workers into new jobs. But this may be starting to change. Late in 1998 Boeing announced plans to lay off more than 48,000 workers—people making good pay at good jobs—as a result of declining demand for its jumbo jets in the Far East and elsewhere around the world. The steel industry has been rocked by imports flooding our market as it seeks to export its way to growth. George Becker, the visionary leader of the Steelworkers Union, fears that tens of thousands of good-paying jobs will be lost if aggressive action isn't taken. U.S. employees will pay the price.

It's not just basic manufacturing that is feeling the impact. The semiconductor industry faces pressure from cheap memory and other chips from overseas. The American Electronics Association announced late in 1998 that many export markets were dropping: Brazil had dropped 8 percent, and exports to Asia were down 12 percent. Pressure from international competition is now being felt in all sectors of the U.S. economy.

It's important to note that businesses are not out to "get" the worker. The truth is that companies are themselves facing enormous pressures. American firms know that if they raise the price of their product someone else—a manufacturer in Singapore, China, Brazil, or Europe—might undersell them. At the same time, they need to keep profit levels up to attract investors to provide the capital for their business operations. That means they have to continually seek productivity gains as well as trim expenses. Often the easiest, quickest way to do that is to cut labor costs. And as the stock market, month after month, reaches new highs, investors have come to demand ever-greater returns. The inevitable result is additional pressure on labor costs.

Of course, many of today's workers are investors as well. Some receive part of their pay in the form of stock options or employee stock ownership plans (ESOPs); others invest in mutual funds for their retirement. Many are finding that even though their salaries are not increasing their paper wealth from investments is. Thus, they may not be demanding large salary increases—simply because they feel wealthier.

In a way, they are more wealthy. But if the stock market drops, they'll be left with little to show for it except, perhaps, a mountain of debt. Millions of consumers have bridged the gap between essentially stagnant salaries and paper wealth with consumption via credit cards. It feels good in the short run, but it's a risky long-term strategy.

During a trip I took to Boston, a friend of mine, Pascalino Columbaro, asked a group of people he knows to take time out of their day to talk with me. I try to do this as often as I can, simply to keep in touch with people's interests, concerns, and needs.

During this particular session, one woman who holds a job as a mental health care worker told me, "It's not the human side of what we do that's valued. It's more the almighty dollar." Though she lives modestly, she said, "I can't afford to live on the salary I make with the debt I have."

Another woman, a former retail clerk at Filene's Basement, chimed in: "Dignity? Forget it. Not only does the company treat you like dirt, so does the public. Everything is valued, but it's not rewarded."

A middle-aged man who'd been making a living as a temporary worker had been sitting quietly throughout the session, listening to what everyone else had to say. He'd been getting increasingly angry, looking for an opportunity to tell his story. Finally he exclaimed, "I work for Blue Cross now, but they don't give me health insurance! And about 20 or 30 percent of the employees are in the same position." He continued: "They treat you like a spare part. We're scared. We can be dumped for no reason. There are no rights."

The erosion of security affects folks at the middle and even the top of the ladder as well. Living standards are stagnant even for many workers with four-year college degrees. Productive employees are being laid off by profitable corporations. And amid economic expansion, we have experienced an unprecedented growth of involuntary part-time work and a steady decline in benefits ranging from health coverage to retirement pensions.

This is the opposite of what America needs in the global information age economy: Instead of more insecure workers, we need more empowered workers. How can U.S. companies compete with world-class speed, efficiency, and quality, with a demoralized, anxious workforce that wonders whether jobs will be there tomorrow?

Of course, we can't go back to some idyllic golden age—if any such age ever really existed. The trends that are squeezing modern workers are powerful ones long in the making: the advent of instantaneous communication linking businesses around the world; the opening of worldwide markets for capital, goods, services, and labor; the triumph of free enterprise in many countries once closed to it; and the emergence of an educated middle-class workforce in dozens of former third world nations. The American worker of the 1950s held a uniquely privileged position thanks in part to a series of happy historical accidents. Those days are gone, probably forever. And on the whole, that's a good thing.

However, too many observers of today's economic landscape—

including many charged with developing government policy—have concluded that Americans must be helpless in the face of economic trends and forces like the ones I've mentioned. That is dead wrong. There's much we can do to influence how the new global economy will treat the working people who fuel its growth. It's the job of our generation to seize that opportunity. Change is inevitable, but economic transition can be more actively managed to achieve an outcome that is more just for all.

For starters, Americans today must dramatically change the relationship between employers and employees. The traditional hierarchical structure that may have been appropriate for the industrial age is now inadequate. Instead, we need more democracy in the workplace, greater access to information by all employees, and more cooperation and collaboration between managers and workers. If we can achieve this, more and more employees will be empowered to "think like owners," putting their heads and hearts into every minute of every workday, as owners do. Such a change will unleash our nation's true potential, helping us not only to maintain our high standard of living but also to lead the world in the same direction.

The defeat of communism has put our economic and political system to the test worldwide. If we can make it work to its full capacity in the face of global competition, it will truly be the system everyone on earth will want to emulate.

# The Responsibilities of Business

One way to characterize periods of history is by examining where society's focus of power lies. In Europe during the middle ages the Church was at the center of power. Gradually, during the centuries of the Reformation and the Enlightenment, national governments took over that role, and kings, parliaments, prime ministers, and presidents established most of the rules and standards that individuals lived by.

Today, with the rise of a global free-market economy, a new shift is occurring. Now businesses are often in the dominant role, operating across national borders and wielding enormous power to affect economies and individuals. When a major corporation shifts capital from one continent to another, it influences more lives, for good or ill, than most acts of legislation.

Some businesses have assumed the mantle of leadership that should accompany such power. Many U.S.-based chemical companies, for example, have adopted codes of conduct that govern their activities wherever they do business. Self-interest is one powerful motivation for such behavior: The chemical disaster that killed thousands in Bhopal, India, years ago opened many eyes to the potential for legal and financial havoc when corporations behave irresponsibly. Yet many in business are driven by a genuine desire to be good corporate citizens in the world. Organizations like Business for Social Responsibility, led by executive Arnold Hiatt, are an example. More businesses must begin to take a similar path—and the governments and peoples of the world must demand that they do so.

In fact, it's time for an open debate about the role businesses play in the world economy. And the place for the debate to begin is here in America—the world's financial and economic leader. Unfortunately, the realities of political power make it difficult to launch such a debate, as events from recent years brought home to me vividly.

In early 1996 a spate of major downsizings, many at apparently healthy and thriving companies, reached a climax in January when communications giant AT&T announced plans to lay off tens of thousands of workers. Shortly thereafter, Republican presidential aspirant Patrick Buchanan spoke out against corporate layoffs. So did then–Secretary of Labor Robert Reich, labeling millions of middle-class Americans the "anxious class." Others spoke out, including Democratic Senators Edward Kennedy and Jeff Bingaman.

I spoke out, too. During the 1950s and 1960s Wall Street rewarded companies that invested in their futures and in the future of the nation. When plans for a new factory were unveiled, investors regarded this as a sign that the company had a good future and that there would be markets for its products for years to come. Share prices rose as a result. Now, just the opposite was happening: Wall Street was rewarding companies for downsizing, plant closings, and massive layoffs; the mark of success was cutting costs so as to boost profits for the next quarter. Neither the stock market nor corporate boards nor company management seemed able to think about long-term growth or the close connection between business success and the prosperity of communities.

I felt that the national outcry against corporate short-sightedness that arose in early 1996 offered our political leadership a rare opportunity to act. We had a chance to turn the personal misfortune of thousands of laid-off workers to the long-term benefit of the nation. For quite some time I had advocated a code of conduct by which U.S. businesses should govern their overseas operations, as well as a series of worker empowerment measures here at home, including pay-for-performance incentives, stock options for employees at all levels, and other efforts to promote "gainsharing" in companies across the country. I hoped that the anger over the AT&T layoffs might provide the spark to ignite a major debate about national business policy.

To my dismay, the White House strongly opposed our efforts. Bob Reich's speech and press interviews sent shock waves through the administration, but the reaction was almost entirely hostile. Indeed, Secretary of the Treasury Robert Rubin made no effort to hide his anger over Reich's statements, and it quickly became clear that the president shared his displeasure.

There were two reasons for the administration's reaction. First, more so than any other recent Democrat, Bill Clinton had embraced the concerns of business owners and managers. The political benefits to Clinton and the party were enormous, and the administration was opposed to opening up any new policy initiatives that would undermine support from business. Since so many business leaders assume—wrongly, I think—that what's good for workers and communities must be bad for the bottom line, they automatically oppose any effort, like ours, to call attention to the larger responsibilities of business.

The second problem was that the message of concern being sounded by me, Reich, and the others ran counter to the administration's agenda. The primary public-relations goal of the White House was to take credit for the rising economy and the jobs it had created. They feared that to talk about those Americans who had been left behind during Bill Clinton's presidency would undermine this positive message.

I wasn't trying to undermine that positive message—far from it. I was proud of what we'd accomplished with Democratic leadership and eager to claim credit for it, which frankly we'd failed to do during the 1994 midterm elections. In large part, I believed Democrats lost control of the House of Representatives in 1994 because of our leadership on the 1993 budget agreement. It was an agreement that called for a measure of pain and sacrifice on the part of many Americans. But that same agreement was the chief accomplishment of the 103rd Congress; it led to the elimination of the crushing budget deficits bequeathed to the nation by the Ronald Reagan–George Bush years and the creation of a budget surplus in 1998.

So neither I nor Bob Reich was interested in hurting the Democratic Party. But I *was* trying to say that we had much more work to do; that though the economy was sound, not all Americans were benefiting as they should.

Those of us who had spoken out in Congress gathered together. Our staffs worked for days to devise a common agenda. After a couple weeks' work, we had a document that called for greater responsibility by all the players: employers, employees, government, and the financial markets. We advocated more retirement security, gainsharing in the workplace, and new efforts to promote productivity and growth.

But the White House put substantial pressure on us to limit our aggressiveness on these important issues. Reluctantly—and unfortunately—we agreed to follow their lead. I felt it was vital to re-elect President Clinton and to try and win back Democratic control of the Congress so as to re-create the partnership of Clinton's first two years. I didn't want to be responsible for undermining the unified message that we had worked so hard to achieve.

I now think the American public could easily have understood an administration claiming credit for the good things it had accomplished while vowing to do even better. Rather than feeding Republican efforts to denigrate the president's achievements, such simple honesty, I believe, would have been appreciated by the public.

We did win one victory. President Clinton agreed to sponsor the White House Conference on Corporate Citizenship. It was a way to showcase some of our most responsible companies as examples of how business should act.

Along the same lines, I'd hoped to create a national award modeled after an Australian program designed to promote "best practices." This program highlighted the activities of Australian companies in creating cooperative relationships between management and labor and promoting high-performance organizations. Companies across the country competed for the honors, and the winners proudly displayed the Best Practices Award logo next to their own. To the public, it was a sign that this was a company you could be proud to do business with. In return, the winners agreed to disseminate information on what they'd done to create a more productive environment and a better workplace.

One construction company won the Best Practices Award by focusing on cross-training their workers. They created what they called a "skills passport," which would enable an electrician, for example, to become licensed as a plumber. The result was that their workers were always in demand as they learned new trades and could operate flexibly on the job site. As you can imagine, the workers cherished the program, and their enhanced skills benefited the company, too.

Back in 1993, I'd begun drafting legislation to emulate the Best

Practices program. I thought it would help spark debate here in the United States about corporate leadership and citizenship. Most important, it could help demonstrate that businesses can do well and do good at the same time. I still think it would be a fine program for the United States. But when the Republicans under Newt Gingrich took control of Congress in 1994, I decided to abandon my efforts to pass legislation to establish it. I was afraid that the Republicans would take the idea and transform it into a vehicle for achieving antilabor goals.

My fears were well-founded. Not only did the Republicans in Congress want to diminish the power of labor; as it turned out, shortly after the Conservatives were elected in Australia, they destroyed their own Best Practices program. Apparently the idea of labor-management cooperation for the benefit of all simply didn't fit their model of employer-employee relations. The concept was a lost opportunity for the United States—one that I'll happily revive when the time is right.

# Stakeholder Economics

I'm sometimes criticized as antibusiness. It's a false charge, of course. Businesses create jobs and help build the national wealth; a healthy economy is dependent on a vibrant, creative, profitable business community, and I've worked for decades to help ensure that we always have one.

At the same time, I do advocate basic rules and standards for business and economic behavior. I believe there must be a floor—a set of minimum standards below which no one is permitted to fall. Wisely designed regulations regarding healthful workplace conditions, protection of the environment, the minimum wage, product safety, and truth in advertising have all promoted increased business activity, a higher standard of living, and a better nation for all. In some quarters it's unfashionable to say a kind word about any form of regulation, but I think only a tiny minority of Americans really want to return to the bad old days of "anything goes" business activity.

However, I reach a little farther than some politicians. I believe that government, in addition to creating a floor, has a role in helping find ways to make America's workplaces better. Many people spend the majority of their waking hours on the job, and they should be working to live, not living to work. The approach I favor has sometimes been described as *stakeholder economics*. It seeks to promote economic growth and opportunity for *all* players in the economy and to reduce the adversarial nature of business-labor relations.

Who or what is a *stakeholder*? It's any individual or group that is affected by a business and, in turn, has an influence on the success or failure of that business. Owners and shareholders, of course, are stakeholders. So are managers and employees. But so are communities and government, and so, in differing ways, are community and government groups. The reality of today's business world is that any smart enterprise needs to operate with *all* of its stakeholders in mind. If you disregard any stakeholder group—for example, by abusing employees, polluting the environment, or defrauding customers—you'll quickly alienate the very people upon whom your success, even survival, ultimately depends. Thus, stakeholder economics seeks to recognize and balance the competing claims of various corporate stakeholders so that win-win decisions can be reached for everyone's benefit.

That is the strategy we need to promote in modern America. Unfortunately, the pressures of today's financial markets often work in exactly the opposite way. Old-fashioned economic theory focuses exclusively on one set of stakeholders: the shareholders who nominally own the business. According to a number of economists, management should strive to increase the value of the company's stock to the exclusion of all other goals. And so powerful have today's capital markets become that many businesses are run with almost that degree of single-mindedness.

I've talked to countless business leaders who want to invest in the long-term health of their companies—for example, by offering training programs for promising workers—but who feel constrained from doing so by the decrees of some whiz kid–stock analyst, focused solely on the short-term bottom line. Too many corporate executives live in terror of a thumbs-down from the denizens of Wall Street. The result, as the former chief financial officer of Levi Strauss once said to me, is that "we spend more time justifying results rather than influencing them."

Sandy Nelson, former head of Inland Steel, told me how hard it was to convince Wall Street that his company's investments in employee training and retraining were worthwhile. Although the firm was showing dramatic increases in quality and productivity, he said, "I have to justify everything to these analysts. And they're only interested in what I'm going to do for them tomorrow, not a year from tomorrow."

We've all seen the stock market gyrate in response to company earnings reports. The logic is often hard to fathom. Sometimes, despite the fact that profits are up, if a company misses some analyst's projection by even as little as a penny per share, the company's stock price plummets. Every experienced investor knows that greed, fear, and other irrational emotions play a powerful role on Wall Street. But it makes no sense to me that these forces should hold the long-term good of American enterprises—and American workers—hostage.

The truth is that people and profits really aren't mutually exclusive. Fred Reichheld, a management consultant in Boston, wrote a best-selling business book some time ago that caught my eye—*The Loyalty Effect*. Fred argues that working to nurture the loyalty of your customers, of your investors, and of your workers will pay rich rewards for everyone. It was one of the first times I've seen someone quantify the intuitive truth that treating people right and focusing on the long-term will actually benefit everyone.

Jack Stack, CEO of Springfield Remanufacturing Holdings Company—a firm I'll have more to say about later—is one of today's visionary business leaders. He's an example of real-life managers putting this new philosophy to work. Jack once told me, "If I can't get every employee, from division heads to janitors, to think about this business every day as I, the owner, do, then I've failed—and we won't reach our full potential, either in terms of profit or of human development."

"Thinking like an owner," Jack went on to explain, has two essential elements: "First, every worker must have sufficient information and decisionmaking power to be highly productive—for customers and for the company. Second, the wealth created must be distributed fairly, not just to leaders and stockholders but also to the workers who helped created it."

Sounds simple? Yes, Jack agrees: "But it's hard to get business leaders to give up the sense of power they get from the old ways of managing."

Make no mistake, we're talking about a new design in the ways businesses are managed and in the way workers think about their jobs. It's based on the recognition that men and women don't work for pay alone but also for the psychic reward that comes from knowing that you're contributing to something that belongs to you: "thinking like an owner." The alternative? Having workers go through their workdays largely brain dead and spirit dead. It's just not good enough anymore.

Some business leaders argue that in the global dog-eat-dog marketplace the only way to meet quarterly profit goals is to drive down "people costs" to meet the foreign competition. This line of reasoning leads to union-busting efforts, downsizing, and flights to third world nations. It's a natural consequence of the assumption that people represent only a cost—a drag on profits to be reduced as much as possible.

But what if people were viewed instead as business's greatest resource? If every employee is part-owner of the enterprise, empowered to do whatever it takes, minute by minute and day by day, to make the enterprise thrive, suddenly the equation looks different. Now, each employee is invited to use every ounce of his or her intelligence, creativity, experience, and knowledge to make better products and services more efficiently. This new approach asks employees to be *human*—in the highest meaning of that word—not cogs in a machine.

And compared to machines, human beings are expensive, even at minimum wage. So it only makes sense for a business to encourage its people to use all their talents on the company's behalf. If all you get from a worker is the efficiency of a machine, everyone—stockholders included—is being shortchanged.

The new, more democratic style of business leadership doesn't mean there will never be downsizing or disputes with unions.

Competition will remain fierce; it demands the utmost of us all. But when workers become owners, common goals emerge for which we all can struggle, rather than fighting one another over slices of a shrinking pie.

Does this all sound too good to be true? I know it's not. In recent years, I've visited dozens of workplaces of all kinds—from factories and coal mines to offices and laboratories—where management and employees work together to improve productivity and quality, places where there is a shared vision and a shared strategy for the future. Everyone knows that there are risks to be faced, but they also know that they're in it together and will sink or swim as a team. Companies ranging from Springfield Remanufacturing, Southwest Airlines, Enterprise Corporation, and Saturn Corporation to Rosenbluth International, Magma Copper, and Drummond Coal—and many others—give life to my view that profits and people aren't mutually exclusive. Good things are happening in manufacturing companies, in service companies, in retail—all across the board. From the Rust Belt to Silicon Valley, there's a quiet renaissance waiting to be ignited.

Clearly there is no one-size-fits-all blueprint for every workplace. Yet there are some common principles shared by businesses that are doing the right thing by all their stakeholders: management that shares its vision with employees; an emphasis on worker training and empowerment as essential to quality; rewards for productivity improvements; and realistic levels of employee security.

Government can do a lot to make these "best practices" more common. We can create incentives for companies to pay workers more to reward productivity gains and encourage improved training and career ladders for frontline workers. We can use government contracting and purchasing to encourage best practices, and we can reform labor law to better protect workers' rights to organize unions and also to promote cooperation between management and labor.

Finally, we can take every opportunity to call attention to the corporate good citizens that demonstrate how fairness to every stakeholder can coexist with exceptional productivity and profitability. Let me tell you about some of them.

# Labor Peace at Magma Copper

Copper mining is one of the toughest jobs in the world, and copper miners are as tough as the work. They're fighters, known for their willingness to settle problems through any means necessary.

In contrast, their employers—the copper-mining companies—have historically viewed miners as deserving of little respect: necessary to the operation, but no more than that. Partly as a result, copper mining was an industry prone to bitter labor-management disputes that often erupted in violence.

In June 1989 the contract between Magma Copper in Arizona and the mineworkers' union was up for renegotiation. Not surprisingly, the company wanted to squeeze the union; the union, predictably, pushed back. Negotiations reached an impasse, and the company decided to play its ace in the hole—hiring replacement workers. The company went so far as to bring in trailers to house replacement miners during the strike. One night, one of the trailers was destroyed by an explosion. Thus began an escalating round of violence on both sides that was all too typical of labor relations in the mining business.

The strike was averted at the last moment and the workers stayed on their jobs, yet Magma Copper continued to suffer from distrust, even hatred, between the miners and management. The episode had left the firm financially troubled, and internal antagonism and distrust threatened to destroy the company.

In 1988, however, Magma Copper had hired a new manager by the name of Burgess Winter. He was a former mining executive from the United Kingdom who had most recently worked in South Africa. Winter now quickly recognized what a predicament the mining company was in, both financially and in terms of labor unrest.

Winter decided that only drastic action could turn around the desperate situation. One day, carrying only a set of the company's account books and a cold case of beer, he marched into the union hall, a place no former manager would ever have dared to enter. As the amazed and suspicious workers gathered around, Winter opened the books and explained, line by line, what the various figures for income and expenses, assets and liabilities meant.

Slowly, the picture of a deeply troubled business emerged. Magma, it was clear, was losing money and in danger of going under. If management and labor couldn't find ways to increase productivity and profits, the mine would have to close. If that happened, Winter made clear, everyone would suffer: The miners and most of the managers would lose their jobs; the company would lose millions of dollars. They were in trouble—but they were in it together.

It was the first time that anyone from company management had reached out with simple honesty to the workers—and the workers responded. When I visited Magma in 1994, cooperative efforts by workers and management had increased the company's productivity to the point where it was the most profitable copper-smelting operation in America. Contrary to previous plans, Magma announced that it would continue production and make additional investments to increase output at one of its local mines because the productivity improvements had returned the mine to profitability. As a result, more than 2,000 miners would keep their jobs, putting food on their families' tables and roofs over their heads. New manager Winter and John Champagne, the company president and a remarkable leader in his own right, were rightfully proud of what they and the workers had accomplished.

I visited the building where the huge trucks that transported the ore were housed. It had once been considered a kind of Siberia; keeping the vehicles up and running was a dirty job that no one wanted to do, and only those workers who'd crossed the wrong manager were assigned the task. Morale, of course, was abysmal, and the quality of the work matched it: At any given time, about half the trucks were broken down awaiting maintenance, forcing miners throughout the operation to scramble for vehicles or just sit and wait, wasting time and money.

When Burgess Winter took over, he cut the number of workers in the vehicle maintenance staff (reassigning them to other jobs in the mine). Then he told the workers that remained, "Now figure out how to get *all* the trucks up and running, and *keep* them running—whatever it takes!" The supervisor who'd been in charge was removed and the position was eliminated. The workers themselves were given the responsibility of meeting the challenge—somehow.

And somehow, they did. Soon enough, the workers pointed with pride to the vehicles—*their* vehicles, they called them. They bragged about how they'd dramatically reduced downtime due to

out-of-commission trucks and therefore increased the mine's productivity yet again. The vehicle maintenance staff no longer com-
prised the mine's outcasts: They now considered themselves an
elite corps of get-it-done problem-solvers. They could clearly see
their vital importance to the whole effort.

When I met with a small group of workers, they told me about
how pleased they were to have put behind them the conflict and
violence that had been Magma's legacy. Now they saw a future for
themselves in copper mining. The head of the union described
how they were working with the company to open a mine overseas. Although a foreign mine might compete with the Arizona
plant, it would make the company stronger financially—and the
U.S. workers now saw that as a benefit to them as well.

Finally, I asked: "What's changed?" One veteran miner, his face
weathered by the elements, his hands as brown and sinewy as old
leather, stood up and spoke for the group, saying simply: "We trust
them."

Such simple words—yet so powerful. The crucial change, of
course, had come when management opened the books—the
books that held the answers to the workers' futures, as well as the
company's. Under the old regime, workers had no way of knowing whether or not the company had a future. Rumor had it that
the mines were running out of ore, and the hoarding of information only deepened the suspicion that the worst must be true. The
simple gesture of trust embodied in the opening of the financial
records had made it possible for management and miners to work
together for the good of all.

Wall Street noticed the difference, too. Magma stock had risen
from a low of $5 per share in 1988 to a new high of $28, creating $2

billion of new wealth for the shareholders. Everyone connected with Magma was winning.

I'd like to say that the happy ending of the Magma Copper story continues to this day. Unfortunately, however, the company's success did it in during the early 1990s. Broken Hill Proprietary (BHP), one of the largest companies in Australia, bought Magma out. Burgess Winter was reassigned. When world copper prices plummeted in 1998, the old ways crept back into the operation, no longer guided by the hand of Winter.

The workers no longer felt as if the company was involving them, and as a result they didn't care so deeply about the company's future. Today, Magma Copper again is struggling. It's a sobering reminder of how easily breakthroughs for the better can be lost without a continually renewed effort.

# Open-Book Management

One of the most exciting workplaces I've been to is Springfield Remanufacturing Company (SRC). It's run by Jack Stack, a man I have gotten to know well and now consider a good friend. Jack has built an exciting future for himself and his employees by focusing on the basics and treating people right, starting with the same "open book" concept that Burgess Winter brought to Magma Copper.

SRC originally grew out of the misfortune that beset the great International Harvester Corporation during the early 1980s. Jack was the manager of an engine-rebuilding operation run by International Harvester in Springfield, Missouri—a grimy, gritty shop where mechanics took apart old engines from farm machinery and heavy equipment and rebuilt them, piece by oily piece. It wasn't glamorous work by any means, but it paid the bills for a lot of local families.

In financial straits, Harvester announced that it was going to close down the Springfield operation. Jack Stack decided that he wanted to buy the business. He and a couple of other managers took out a bank loan and sank the cash into the company, now rechristened the Springfield Remanufacturing Company.

However, as soon as Jack studied the cash-flow projections and other financial documents of the business, he knew how much trouble the place was in: Merely doing business the same way wouldn't be good enough. If SRC was going to work, he needed to get the employees to understand what they were up against. Not only was his job on the line, but so were theirs.

Jack made the same radical decision Burgess Winter made: He decided to open the books to the employees to show them exactly where things stood and what it would take to make it all work. He didn't hide anything—where the profits were, how much the firm was worth, he even told everyone how much cash was available on a daily basis.

Like the miners at Magma Copper, the SRC employees responded—in spades. What started out in 1983 as a single facility with 180 employees has now grown into 23 related companies employing more than 1,200 people. Although Jack originally opened the company's books out of desperation, the universal sharing of financial results and plans has evolved into a fundamental philosophy of the company. SRC's success has started a new business trend: open-book management. It's based on the simple yet powerful understanding that when everyone understands the business and how the business works, they will make a difference because they know what they need to do to succeed.

On my first visit to SRC, I toured one of the new companies that grew out of the original operation. It's understood that whenever SRC finds a new line of business that its employees are interested in, they'll investigate and decide together whether it represents a real opportunity. If it does, they'll start a new company. The CEO of this new company had originally been the janitor in the original operation and had grown through the organization to lead a unit employing fifty people. Recently this CEO took a position at another one of SRC's companies so as to give his assistant a chance to move up the ladder. She was thrilled to have the new opportunity and it's a tribute to the kind of people-centered management that is evident everywhere you go at SRC.

Every week, all the employees at each of the operations gather in the "huddle room," where everyone participates in goal-setting, evaluation, and analysis. The room is lined with blackboards where the employees post all the crucial numbers—cash flow, orders, accounts receivable, and so on. Each employee comes armed with a notebook filled with information and analysis, much like pro football players with the game plan for Sunday's matchup. They examine and discuss the figures constantly to determine whether or not the company is achieving its plan for the year. They make adjustments as necessary. And everyone, from secretary to chief financial officer, is a part of the process.

The analysis comes easily now, but it wasn't always that way. Each new employee at SRC is trained in how to read an income statement and a balance sheet, and every week people learn something new about financial ratios, sharpening their eyes for potential problems and opportunities on the shop floor. They're rewarded for the extra responsibility. In addition to a base salary, each employee is eligible for bonuses and stock based on achieving goals set jointly by management and workers—although at SRC the distinction between the two groups is a lot less marked than at most companies.

The day I first visited, the company was about three weeks away from the end of a quarter. As I walked around, I asked each employee I met how the company was doing. Every one of them knew—down to the dollar—how close they were to their quarterly target. What's more, they were pumped up about it. It was almost like being in a football locker room at halftime, with victory in sight.

A woman in shipping talked about what she was doing to reduce costs in her department so as to add to the bottom line—the company's bottom line *and* her own. When I stopped to talk to a man rewiring motors, he explained how he'd found a way to reuse some of the scrap wire, thereby cutting costs while keeping the product quality well above the competition. These are typical SRC stories. Every employee knows he or she has a role to play, and no one wants to let the team down.

There have been countless management fads in the past, from "quality circles" to "reengineering." But I think that open-book management is more than just another temporary fashion. It's an overall approach to corporate governance that treats the employees like co-owners of the business who have to make the sacrifices and take on the burdens that any owner assumes. To put it another way, it treats workers like fellow-citizens in a democracy where everyone has a responsibility to participate in and contribute to a successful future.

Far from being some kind of idealistic do-good scheme, open-book management is also eminently practical. It's based on the hard truth that most employees know more about what they're doing than anyone else; the trick is to allow them to use that knowledge to become as creative and productive as possible. In most businesses, employees are never given enough "big picture" financial information to see how their efforts fit in the total picture, nor are they asked to take responsibility to use their knowledge to make things run better. Too many supervisors don't care about what the employees think, and they don't ask. Any communication is one-way communication, so the business never taps the wisdom and experience of the employees. Open-book management turns that around. It energizes scores or hundreds of minds, not just the handful of those who've been anointed as managers.

Open-book management isn't going to be practiced everywhere. To many employers, it's a daunting, even frightening concept. Jack Stack talks about how hard it was for him to give up control of the books, to share the information with the employees: Control of the facts had always been at the core of his power as a manager. But once he took that leap of faith—forced into it, admittedly, by the company's problems—he realized how hard it would be to ever go back. People begin to *expect* access to information, and if you take it away, you're likely to have a revolt on your hands. Just as in politics, democracy in business is infectious—and difficult to kill once it has truly taken root.

# Reinventing the Car Business

Saturn Corporation in Springhill, Tennessee, has been one of the most widely studied business experiments in recent years. It originated in an attempt by General Motors to create a new kind of car company. Working together, management and labor designed the factory, the strategic plan, the management system, the employment contract, and just about everything else related to Saturn. During its early years, Saturn was a huge success. Today, Saturn is having trouble maintaining that success over the long term. Both the initial success and the current problems are instructive.

Over the years, I've visited automobile factories across the country and around the world. I always ask for the opportunity to meet and talk with both workers and managers. A company's success, I've found, is determined by more than just how "hot" its products are. If the system for producing those products is not up to par, then in the long term there will be trouble, and only meeting the people behind the business can tell you that.

Here in the United States, when a visitor is met at the factory door by managers *and* employees, you can usually tell that it's a well-run company. That's the approach I saw at Saturn. By contrast, at other General Motors facilities, I was met by managers only. It took a special request for me to meet with ordinary employees, usually behind closed doors in a conference room where the managers knew they just weren't welcome. The adversarial quality of labor relations there is obvious, as it is in far too many companies throughout the country.

Saturn is different. In fact, it is often hard to tell who is a manager and who is an hourly employee. You feel it walking through the front door and everywhere you go. Touring the factory, you see cars traveling the assembly line on "ergonomic pallets." Each employee can raise or lower the car to a height that lets him or her work without having to bend way over or reach abnormally high—actions that in most factories lead eventually to needless fatigue, stress, and injury. Remember, at Saturn the employees were involved from day one in designing the facility; this is a small example of the resulting benefits.

Saturn's people-management methods are unusual, too. Teams of up to fifteen people meet periodically to decide how they will meet production goals set by management. Employees generally work ten-hour days, four days per week, with rotating day and night shifts. At the end of a three-week cycle, they get five consecutive days off.

The Saturn mystique doesn't end at the factory door. Consider how Saturn selected the dealers for its new retail network. As usual, company managers interviewed prospective dealers, but handpicked auto-assembly employees sat in on the interviews as well. Once the dealers were at work, assemblers would periodically visit the dealerships incognito, posing as car buyers to see how "their" cars were being sold to the public.

Many Saturn buyers have developed an almost religious zeal about the company, much like aficionados of Harley-Davidson motorcycles. Several years ago, Saturn held a reunion for its car buyers at the Saturn plant in Springhill. Thousands of Saturn owners showed up for the two days of festivities. Yes, even customers can be company stakeholders—and if you treat them right, they can think and act like owners, becoming your products' best salespeople in the process.

Some time ago, I'm told, Saturn ran into a problem. It simply did not have enough salespeople to keep up with showroom traffic. So the company wrote a group of Saturn owners and invited them to come into the showroom for a day to answer questions from the public—without pay. More than *half* of those contacted were happy to do so. Stakeholder economics can pay!

Saturn has faced repeated and continuing trials. The commitment of General Motors to the Saturn experiment has been called into question several times, and corporate leaders have been reluctant at times to provide the capital needed to expand Saturn's operations and product line. At times, the commitment of the workers to the Saturn system has been called into question and the workers have installed new leadership. The Saturn experiment is still evolving: Only time will tell whether or not this experiment succeeds.

Ironically, General Motors, which spawned the exciting Saturn experiment, has the worst overall labor relations of America's automakers. General Motors has tried to isolate the Saturn experiment, not allowing similar progressive methods to be implemented in its other facilities across the country. Although the General Motors labor contract is roughly equivalent to that of Ford and Chrysler, the company says that it can't survive under the existing contract.

Unlike Ford and Chrysler, General Motors has refused to recognize that it needs to develop high-performance work organizations and abandon traditional labor-relations approaches. Ford and Chrysler don't do everything right. Yet they've moved forward at a much faster pace.

# The Worker Comes First

M any of the progressive business changes that have been studied and reported widely are found in manufacturing companies. That's because it's often easier to quantify the gains that occur. You can, for example, look at the number of products produced per hour and measure their quality using numbers. Employee rewards can then be based on those numbers. By contrast, service quality is harder to define.

However, one of the best current examples of the kind of workplace we need to promote for the future exists at Rosenbluth International, headquartered in Philadelphia. The CEO of the company, Hal Rosenbluth, has, in just a couple of decades, seen his travel agency's revenues grow from $20 million to $4.5 billion!

Before I visited Hal, I took the time to read his book *The Customer Comes Second*. Hal says that if you treat your employees right—if you listen to them, treat them well, include them in "vision-setting"—they will attract and keep customers. Thus, putting employees first leads to satisfied customers and a growing business.

Hal's idea appears to be working. When I visited his company, it was the first and only time I have found a company leader who trusted his employees so completely that he didn't even meet me at the door. He left it up to them to take me around, to introduce me to their coworkers, to talk over lunch about where they had been and where they were going. Only at the end of my visit did I spend time with Hal. Some might have been insulted; I viewed it as the ultimate sign of Hal's respect for his employees.

At Rosenbluth International, employees may sit in on virtually any management meeting. Lists of the upcoming meetings are posted in the hallways so that employees can schedule time to participate. In open-book style, workers have information about where the business is going and can evaluate how they can participate in promoting its future.

Over lunch, one person—call him Gary—commented, "You know, not everyone can be a superstar at work." At Rosenbluth International, that's not necessarily a problem. In fact, Gary explained, they didn't always try to recruit those with the slickest résumés. Superstar types, they'd found, were often unable to work well with others as a team. Accustomed to getting ahead through individual effort—rather than by promoting the interests of the organization—superstars tended to put themselves first. By contrast, the most valued employees at Rosenbluth believed that they were all in it together. The surprising result: Fewer "lone ranger" talents lead to more outstanding overall results for the company.

Later, the staff member who hosted us for the day brought me to Rosenbluth International's Network Operations Center—a high-tech command post lined with rows of television screens in a video wall and outfitted with banks of computers and phones. The center's purpose is to protect the interests of the company's clients who are traveling every hour of the day. Rosenbluth International staffers track worldwide weather conditions to see whether they have to reroute clients around ice storms or floods; they check telephone traffic to determine whether they are being prompt in responding to calls; they even monitor State Department warnings about international trouble spots.

One screen was particularly important to me: employee satisfaction. It reported the latest figures from the worker surveys that are constantly being done at Rosenbluth, providing an early-warning system in the event morale anywhere in the company might dip. As Hal shows in his book, when the staff suffer—from burnout, overwork, unsafe or uncomfortable conditions, or lack of management support—service suffers next, and profits inevitably follow suit. He's determined that won't happen at Rosenbluth International. It became clear that "the customer comes second" isn't just a slogan, it's a real mind-set and a highly effective way of doing business.

Hal's own story is an interesting one. His great-grandfather founded the business, and the leadership had been passed to Hal's father, who ran it while Hal was growing up. Originally, Hal had had no interest in taking over. But shortly after leaving college he found himself working the phones at Rosenbluth Travel (the former name of the company) alongside other young staffers. He quickly noticed that when one of the workers was swamped with calls none of the others jumped in to help out. Wondering why, he invited the crew out for a beer after work one night and asked them to explain their problems on the job—as well as possible solutions. He gathered a wealth of great ideas, which he used to improve the system and mold the group, over time, into a close-knit, mutually supportive team. Hal's uniquely person-centered management style was born.

Today, much of Rosenbluth International's telephone support work is handled from facilities in South Dakota. Why South Dakota? Hal explained why. He happens to own a farm in that state, and he noticed during his visits to other family farms that the people he met were able to perform almost any job on the farm independently. At the same time, they routinely pitched in to help one another when the work required it, even among neighboring farms. "That's the kind of work ethic we want and have at our company," Hal concluded.

# Taking a Chance on Change

In most of today's forward-thinking businesses, there is one common factor: a corporate leader who devotes himself or herself to change; a leader willing to gamble on employees' caring not just about their wages but about their work. It is not easy to gamble like that. Leaders who do are often opposed by their investors, by middle management, and, indeed, by employees. Yet as difficult as it is, change is necessary if we are to succeed.

Corporate leaders often tell me that the real problem is the unions—that union leaders promote conflict because it benefits them. According to this line of thinking, when employees and management work together, there's no need for a union. Thus, union leadership has a vested interest in making sure that cooperation is impossible.

But in many of the progressive companies I've visited, union leadership has helped to promote change. Often, they put their own jobs at risk. At Magma Copper, I asked Burgess Winter whether the union had helped or hurt his ability to institute change. He said, "We couldn't have done it without the union." The union provided the structure for communicating with all the workers, and the union leadership's acceptance of the changes helped instill trust among the employees.

Coming from a union household, I've always been a strong supporter of unions. Some of our greatest accomplishments—Social Security, Medicare, civil rights, and other advances—have been achieved with the help of unions. Unions represent only a small portion of the private-sector workforce, and a declining one at that. Relying on unions alone to gain advances for workers isn't the answer. Furthermore, unless labor and management are openly and honestly sharing ideas and information, neither side can hope to truly change the workplace for the better. Thus, what is necessary is promoting change from the top down *and* from the bottom up. At the same time, until we develop systemic approaches that bring about real change, unions are often the only backstop that workers can rely on to protect their interests.

Far too many companies that seek to promote the interests of all stakeholders rely on the vision of one or a few corporate leaders. When these leaders depart, or when tough times inevitably come, their changes are put to the test. Unfortunately, then, far too many enterprises revert back to the old ways of thinking. The only real exception appears to be those companies that are privately owned and, therefore, somewhat immunized from market pressures coming from Wall Street, the big banks, and other sources of investment capital.

The question, then, is how to promote real, lasting change that is not dependent on the benevolence of a small group of leaders and that applies on a nationwide basis, not just company by company. You can't force these kinds of systemic changes through the power of government. We're simply not smart enough to know what every business ought to do. And things change too quickly for government to develop rules that are flexible enough.

There is, however, a role for government in setting some basic standards and rules. Government has passed laws concerning minimum wages and maximum work hours, health and safety laws, and laws regulating pensions and health care. All of these laws should be fully and faithfully implemented. There is also a role for government in setting ground rules for competition to alleviate the constant downward pressure on wages, salaries, benefits, and working conditions that a state-by-state "race to the bottom" would bring.

I've long advocated a code of conduct for businesses that sets some basic guidelines in these areas. Businesses that adopt and follow the code would be eligible for certain governmental benefits. For example, eventually, federal contracts over some minimum dollar level should be awarded preferentially to companies that offer all their workers basic pension and health care coverage. Such a rule would let businesses know that they don't have to cut back on the health or retirement security of their employees in order to make competitive bids for federal contracts. A similar approach could be used to keep frequent and persistent violators of federal labor, environmental, and health and safety laws from doing business with the government. Gradually, as more and more companies seek to achieve specified goals in order to qualify for government contracts, these goals would be transformed from federal standards into societal ones.

I'm an advocate of pay-for-performance plans to help address inadequate compensation. Our leading business schools often promote the short-term approach to management rather than a long-term approach that involves cooperative vision-setting and investment in people. *The Wall Street Journal* reported how a business school student viewed it: "Why should we reward you people with bonuses? You're like gerbils, running around in a wheel in a cage. Why should we give you more pellets?" It's a common attitude—but a destructive one.

Instead, employees should share in both the risks and the rewards of a business. Abuses clearly are possible; a few owners simply see pay-for-performance as a way to exact more and more work out of their employees. But where it is properly designed and implemented, it can be a real success for employers and employees alike. Government incentives should encourage such plans.

We also need standards regarding training and retraining for workers. Technology and business are changing at an accelerating rate, and we need to make sure that everyone has the skills to keep pace. The smartest firms know that investments in training and retraining help the bottom line. Motorola, for example, estimates that it earns $30 for every $1 invested in employee training. Several years ago, Senator Ted Kennedy and I introduced legislation to mandate that a minimum 1 percent of payroll be dedicated to training and retraining of employees at all levels. Such a rule would help ensure that companies don't cut back on training for competitive reasons; if everyone had to make minimum expenditures, it would eliminate the disincentive to spending the money. And these expenditures would be tax-deductible to companies.

Clearly, unlike some on the Republican side of the aisle, I'm not advocating abandoning government regulations. But I *am* advocating a more balanced approach to working *with* business. Just as with management and labor, we also need to minimize the hostility between business and government. It's time to develop a better partnership—one where each side demands something of the other. After all, sometimes the country's bottom line is different from the corporate bottom line.

None of this means having a paternalistic government—far from it. President Clinton was right when he said, "The era of big government is over." But there remains a role for government. For example, if we want to enhance retirement security, we need to promote savings through incentives for individuals and companies. And in health care, we need to expand coverage not by giving government a larger stick to wield over business but by expanding the use of carrots.

## Change from the Bottom Up

Finally, not all corporate change need be driven by top management. There are examples of line workers and midlevel managers who have helped change the culture of a company from the bottom up. At Ford Motor Company, midlevel managers created many of the worker participation programs that were eventually adopted by the top leadership of the entire corporation. Similarly, at U.S. Repeating Arms in New Haven, Connecticut, I'm told employees crafted a new partnership agreement that enabled them to redesign the workplace, leading to unprecedented improvements in quality and productivity.

It's not easy to do, but line workers and midlevel managers can help promote democratization of the workplace even before the top leadership of a firm sees the light. Here are some ideas for concrete steps you may want to try where you work.

- Study the actions taken at Ford and other companies where line workers and midlevel managers brought about changes in employee participation and responsibility. Can these same steps work in your company?

- Talk with fellow employees about changes you can make to improve the quality and productivity of your workplace. Start small: A modest, documented improvement in one corner of a company can lead to bigger changes throughout the firm.

- Speak to your immediate supervisor or union steward about the new style of democratic, cooperative management. Identify elements of this approach that can work for your company— then give them a try.

- Read one or more of the fine books about the new management, such as Jack Stack's *The Great Game of Business*, and pass them along to your colleagues. Nothing is more encouraging than a road map showing how change has worked in the real world.

Make no mistake: We in government are involved in the same quest as millions in the private sector. The program for "reinventing government" at the federal level, which has dramatically streamlined bureaucracy through employee empowerment and simplification of procedures, is a good example, as are other programs at state and local levels and in the U.S. military. Much good has been done, but more work remains.

## Repairing the Frayed Safety Net

B usinesses need the tools to compete in a world economy. Shackling American business with unrealistic and burdensome regulations that only undermine our ability to compete will ultimately prove self-destructive, as more and more companies will simply pull up stakes and move elsewhere.

At the same time, we must establish some basic standards and rules both for the global economy and for how we deal with economic issues here at home. One of those basic standards is our minimum wage.

My thinking about the minimum wage starts with this premise: *No full-time worker should have to live in poverty.* If you work hard and follow the rules, you deserve a decent life. You may not get rich, but you should have dignity and the ability to provide for yourself and your family.

Unfortunately, during the past few decades, our adjustments in the minimum wage have been so few and so inadequate that inflation has greatly outstripped them. It's almost impossible to live on a minimum-wage salary in most parts of the United States today. Yet 10 million workers have to try.

In 1996, we passed an increase in the minimum wage that went a long way toward restoring its value. It was one of the toughest political fights of recent years.

A majority of Republicans opposed the increase—this despite the fact that most employers, because of the current tight labor market, were already paying their entry-level workers more than the minimum wage. Some conservatives believe so strongly in the autonomy of the free market that they oppose virtually all legal standards as applied to business: the minimum wage, rules about worker safety, food-purity regulations, you name it. Since they can't muster the votes to abolish the minimum wage altogether, they whittle away at its value by fighting any increase. Dick Armey, the Republican Majority Leader in the House, promised to oppose an increase in the minimum wage "with every fiber of my being." He almost won the fight. Joining with small-business lobbyists in Washington, he was able to bottle up an increase and prevent it from being voted on for a long, long time. Eventually, we forced the vote and passed a modest increase.

Much more is needed. We've introduced legislation calling for an additional two-step increase in the minimum wage—to $6.15 per hour by the year 2000. Even that is only a start. Think about this: If you worked for the minimum wage forty hours per week, every week of the year, you'd earn only $12,792 per year *after* our proposed increase! Imagine trying to raise a family on that amount. We need to support efforts that are now starting at the state and local levels to promote a true "living wage," including adjustments for local economic conditions. (It costs more to live in San Francisco than in rural Tennessee; wages may need to reflect that.)

Raising wages does more than help someone buy food or pay for shelter. Remember the Republican nostrum of the 1980s, supply-side economics? I'm a believer in *demand-side* economics. Raising wages increases the buying power of American workers, and that's good for the entire country. And that increased demand will put more people to work, producing the food, clothing, and other goods and services that the working poor and near-poor are eager to afford. That can't help but be healthy for business, too.

The Economic Policy Institute in Washington, D.C., studied the effects of the last minimum-wage increase. It found that both low-wage workers and the overall economy benefited. Contrary to the claims of some doomsayers, few job losses were found. In fact, the American economy has generated more than 7 million new jobs since the first installment of the latest minimum wage increase went into effect.

Another group that has fallen off the ladder to the good life— at least temporarily—are those who receive welfare. And they, too, like minimum-wage workers, have suffered during recent years by becoming a political football for others.

When Bill Clinton ran for the presidency in 1992, his promise to "end welfare as we know it" was a huge crowd-pleaser. No wonder: The welfare system had long been, in the minds of many, a symbol of government waste and, indeed, of government tolerance for those who refused to help themselves. Images painted by Ronald Reagan and Newt Gingrich of "welfare queens"—people supposedly living high on the hog from welfare payments—had passed into folklore, though few real cases were ever uncovered.

Hostility toward the welfare system was also a function of an economy that was not producing good enough results for average, hard-working Americans. The idea that some people were getting government checks every month for doing nothing while most people were scrambling every day just to pay the bills caused understandable resentment.

In truth, of course, most people on welfare always would have preferred a job with decent pay and benefits that would allow them and their families to live in dignity without public assistance. But some couldn't find jobs because of physical or psychological problems, whereas for many others the only jobs available paid the minimum wage and offered no benefits at all. They'd be better off on welfare.

I met a woman in Massachusetts—I'll call her Debra—a single mom whose story could be replicated many times over. Debra had left the welfare rolls to get a job, but as a result she and her family were no longer covered by Medicaid. Since her new job offered no health benefits, Debra was actually putting her children at risk by entering the workforce. The choice was eating her up. Debra lived in constant fear that her children would get sick and she wouldn't be able to afford their care.

By the time Bill Clinton took office, the demand for welfare reform had become an almost unstoppable tide. And though there was enormous controversy over how to implement welfare reform, almost all Americans agreed that welfare should not be permanent and that welfare recipients should be required and assisted to go to work to support their families.

I worked hard with the president and his administration to forge a Democratic approach to welfare reform around which the party could unite. For a time, we were successful. Working with members of a conservative coalition led by Congressman Nathan Deal, we put together a plan that garnered the support of almost the entire House Democratic Caucus.

Unfortunately, the Republican majority in the House instead forced through a plan that drove a knife into the heart of welfare reform. Essentially, the Republican bill told welfare recipients, "You must go to work to support your families like all other Americans. But when you do, you won't have the same protections enjoyed by all other American workers." It denied people moving from welfare to work crucial protections under the Fair Labor Standards Act, including the minimum wage, as well as other federal laws that ensure the dignity of work in America.

Republicans also told welfare recipients who participate in so-called workfare programs that they are not considered "employees" under the law, thereby jeopardizing coverage under the civil rights laws that protect all employees from discrimination in the workplace.

Such unfairness isn't a matter of concern only to the people directly affected. It hurts every employee when this nation tolerates the creation of any second-class workers. That's why I had to oppose the Republican welfare-reform bill. As much as I wanted to change our broken welfare system, the Republican bill didn't do enough to help and protect vulnerable workers and their families.

Ironically, the final bill that Congress passed and the president signed was both too weak on the work requirements that should have been its fundamental purpose and too tough on the innocent children who will end up suffering when their parents cannot find jobs. According to the nonpartisan Urban Institute, more than 1 million children may be forced into poverty because of this bill. We could have done a lot better—for our children and for ourselves.

Supporters of the welfare bill point to the fact that the number of cases on the welfare rolls has fallen dramatically during recent years. Unfortunately, we really don't know what has happened to all those people. The welfare-reform law did not require that individuals be tracked to determine how they fare. Surely some of those now denied assistance have found jobs and have lifted themselves up. But many may have simply vanished into a sort of economic limbo—homeless, jobless, out of school, surviving through handouts, petty crime, or dangerous and poorly paid work in the so-called underground economy.

My real fear is that when the economic boom falters—as inevitably it must—the changes we've made in the welfare system will put millions of kids and families at risk. A slowing economy puts the greatest pressure on workers at the low end of the income scale, and the new work requirements could run headlong into the fact that more and more people will be pursuing fewer and fewer jobs. The downward pressure on wages and benefits this will produce can only worsen the strains on every family's finances and standard of living. Unless we do something now, we may find ourselves with a bigger welfare problem than ever.

# The Changing Path to Retirement Security

**M**oney is now one of the best-selling magazines in America—with good reason. People are increasingly fixated on how they're going to survive in today's economy and prepare for a decent retirement. Polls show that an increasing percentage of people are turning to the business section of their morning newspaper before checking sports or their favorite cartoon. They're tracking their mutual funds and stock investments as avidly as my Dad used to follow Stan Musial's exploits on the baseball diamond.

Times have changed. Years ago, many people took a job after graduation and retired from the same company forty or forty-five years later. They felt secure about receiving a pension that would allow them to live decently in retirement—not cruising the seven seas, mind you, but at least with some well-deserved leisure after a lifetime of hard work.

Today, the old "defined benefit plans," which promised retirees a predictable income, have given way to "defined contribution plans," at the mercy of stock and bond markets and the overall economy. And as workers move more frequently from one job to another—by design or necessity—they're often ineligible for *any* company pension plan. The burden of retirement security falls more and more on the shoulders of the individual worker.

There's a hodgepodge of retirement vehicles out there in which people can invest for the future—individual retirement accounts (IRAs), Keogh plans, 401(k) plans, and others. The real question, of course, is whether people have enough disposable income to save. It's an individual problem, but as an entire generation of baby boomers approaches retirement during the early years of the twenty-first century, it will become a greater and greater societal problem as well.

Part of the answer lies in fixing the weaknesses of the private pension system. We need to find ways to improve the portability of retirement accounts and to shorten vesting periods. We want people to be able to save for their retirement steadily over time rather than in fits and starts. People should also be able to continually roll over their retirement accounts as they move from job to job, giving them control over as well as access to their retirement funds.

The other half of the answer involves Social Security, the foundation of our nation's retirement system. It was created in 1935 as part of Franklin Roosevelt's New Deal to provide a backstop against poverty. At the time, more than half of America's elderly were living in poverty. Today, the figure is about 10 percent. Social Security represents one of the most important and successful peacetime initiatives in our nation's history.

Social Security has also helped ensure that a worker's disability doesn't result in a one-way ticket to the poorhouse or to abject dependency. Three-quarters of workers rely on it as their sole insurance for potential disability, and millions are helped under this provision.

Social Security was never designed to be a retiree's sole source of income. And in the current debate about how to strengthen the system, we should not impose that burden upon it. Yet we must not forget that two-thirds of retirees get a majority of their income from Social Security. For many people, Social Security is all that stands between them and poverty.

Again, social changes must be recognized and taken into account. A century ago, it was common for the elderly to move into their children's homes to be taken care of, financially and in other ways. In some cases, the result was a happy one for all concerned; in other cases, friction, strain, and anxiety over being a "burden" were produced. Today, thanks in part to Social Security, millions of the elderly have unheard-of independence, dignity, and freedom. And as a result, so do their families. A working family can follow career opportunities to another city or state without fretting over Mom; she's probably living comfortably in a retirement community or a place of her own in Florida or Arizona. If our grandparents' generation had the imagination, boldness, and ingenuity to construct a system that has done so much to reduce poverty during the past sixty years, surely we can manage the fine-tuning necessary to ensure its continued success.

Ironically, one of the reasons the Social Security system is under financial pressure today is precisely because it's been so successful. In tandem with Medicare, Social Security has given the elderly the ability to live a decent life with adequate health care. As a result, they're living longer, our nation's percentage of elderly citizens continues to grow, and the costs of both Social Security and Medicare increase accordingly.

Lately we've become accustomed to the stock market hitting new highs almost on a daily basis. It's natural that millions have been turning to Wall Street as their vehicle of choice for retirement saving; according to some statistics, more than half of the population invests in the stock market in some way.

In general, it's a sound strategy. Decades of statistics show that in the long run stock prices overall grow faster and more reliably than any other form of investment. And increasing our nation's savings rate—currently one of the lowest in the world—is all to the good, both for preparing individuals for their own futures as well as for providing the capital that businesses need in order to expand and grow.

But we need to remember that stock values go down as well as up. Even as the overall market is rising, specific companies and mutual funds may crash, wiping out thousands of individual investors in the process. And in a prolonged bear market, the entire market may fall so far that it takes years to recover. Those who retire before the recovery may simply be out of luck.

Furthermore, in today's tightly interwoven global economy, when one nation catches a cold, others start sneezing. So far, the U.S. economy has been able to weather the recent storms buffeting nations in Asia, Latin America, and the Pacific Rim, but it may not always be so. The stock market, in short, is no foolproof source of retirement security.

That's where a foundation program like Social Security comes in. A strong Social Security system actually gives us the opportunity to take risks elsewhere. Think of Social Security as it was always intended—as an insurance system; knowing that it will be there allows us to invest in stocks, bonds, and other investment vehicles with the hope that we'll do well and without having to fear utter destitution should we make a bad pick or two. It allows us to couple a universal system of support with individual responsibility and entrepreneurship.

As I write, Congress is again debating the future of the Social Security system. It's important that we understand exactly what the problem is before we commit ourselves to a final set of answers. We Americans are an impatient lot; we sometimes demand a quick fix for a problem that has been decades in the making. That may be the case with Social Security.

We face a looming shortfall at some point in the future. It's a difficult challenge, but not an imminent crisis. We'll need to take some prudent steps to ensure that the integrity of the system will be guaranteed for current and future retirees well into the twenty-first century. The current federal budget surplus, if dedicated largely to Social Security, can make our task far easier than it would be otherwise.

We also need to find new and imaginative ways to strengthen our national program of saving and investing for the future. Individual accounts can be part of the answer. But they should be voluntary and a supplement to Social Security, not a replacement for it. The approach that President Clinton announced in his 1999 State of the Union address, in which incentives would be created to facilitate voluntary supplemental individual stock market accounts, is a good basis for starting the debate.

# Free Trade in the Postwar World

International trade may be the issue most people identify me with. Unfortunately, it's one of those issues often viewed in simplistic, black-and-white terms. As we all know, the truth is usually best depicted in shades of gray.

In debates about trade, I've been called a protectionist, an isolationist, and worse. Truth is, it's often easier for people to apply labels than to listen to what you have to say. The media helps reduce most debates to simple sound bites. A study of the 1998 California gubernatorial election found that coverage of the candidates on the nightly TV news had fallen to just thirty seconds. And between 1992 and 1996, television coverage of candidates in the presidential elections had dropped by 44 percent. It's hard to say what you believe in that amount of time; you're often stuck with a quick, catchy phrase that doesn't really do justice to your position and beliefs. And when dealing with an "unsexy" topic like trade, the media's attention span is especially short.

Given these obstacles, one of my greatest successes in the Congress may have been my efforts to define and explain the issues surrounding world trade. I've tried to describe for people the kind of economic relationship we should seek with other countries. We know we have to compete in the global economy, but we want that competition to be fair. Fairness is a concept that lies deep in our national psyche and in the most basic terms. *Fairness*—that's what free trade is all about.

Yet many people don't fully recognize how the free trade debate has broadened and deepened during recent years. Since the end of the Cold War, it has become increasingly obvious that we cannot have successful capitalism around the world unless we are able to spread the infrastructure upon which capitalism relies—the rule of law, human rights, labor rights, governmental transparency, and other fundamentals that we in the United States take for granted. It certainly took me a long time to understand this. Ten years ago, it had never occurred to me that a democracy could not have a positive economic relationship with a totalitarian state. Today, I see that very clearly. In fact, there has been a natural and important progression on the trade issue for me. It began during the early 1980s, when I was one of a group of young members of Congress known as the "Atari Democrats," which also included people like Bill Bradley and Gary Hart. We shared the belief that our nation's economic policymakers were not considering the long-term policies needed to ensure a high and rising standard of living for our people. And I believed that we were continually blinded by our adherence to the single guiding principle of containing communism.

This doesn't mean that I wanted us to be soft on defense—far from it. But it became clear to me that though Russia was clearly a military threat we were failing to address the growing economic threats we faced. As defense budgets grew under Democratic and Republican presidents alike, we failed to recognize the problems posed by the increasing economic power of some of our allies.

During the early postwar years, we focused on helping the devastated nations of Europe and Asia to recover economically. This program, as embodied especially in the Marshall Plan, worked brilliantly. Out of the ruins of World War II, we helped build economic powerhouses. Germany and Japan led this effort, developing industrial models that relied heavily on government support and guidance. Japan was direct in its advocacy of this centralized, government-led model. In fact, Japan's Ministry of Trade and Industry periodically published a comprehensive plan indicating which industries it intended to favor, selecting industries it felt would yield the greatest long-term economic benefit for the nation. High-technology, aerospace, and other industries were singled out for support and nurturing in this way—"picking winners and losers" in a way governments aren't supposed to do in capitalist countries.

Germany followed much the same model in a more subtle way. And as in Japan, the integration of the financial sector (especially the banks) to ensure that long-term, competitively priced financial assistance would always be obtained for favored companies helped fuel the efforts. From the ashes of World War II, these and many other countries were able to rebuild, retool, and reignite growth.

We benefited, too. We promoted postwar recovery because we believed that an economically developed Japan and Germany, with increasingly intertwined relations with their former adversaries, would be important factors in ensuring stability and peace. This, in turn, would help us in containing communism, as the economic benefits that would result would dissuade people from rejecting capitalism. It all developed much as we hoped. By the 1980s, varied brands of capitalism were thriving throughout Western Europe and in much of Asia, and communism was on the retreat—in truth, we now know, on its last legs.

But we had a huge blind spot in our postwar economic approach. We assumed that other countries would adopt the same model of capitalism that we did—including our staunch belief in the mutual benefits of free trade. We were wrong. Although Japan, Germany, and the other new economic powers reaped the benefits of the U.S. approach—especially our dedication to maintaining open markets for the products they produced—they did not engage in two-way free trade. The gates too often swung open in one direction only. And some developing countries adopted a form of "crony capitalism," in which economic benefits were enjoyed mainly by those at the top.

And we permitted this to happen. It may sound arrogant to say this, but during the early years after World War II the United States had a golden opportunity to shape the direction our former enemies took. An aide once gave me a copy of a letter from the Tokyo

Provisional Government to General Douglas MacArthur shortly after the war ended. It was written on an old typewriter with misspellings and individual letters appearing in odd places at times. In the letter, the Japanese asked for MacArthur's permission to create a domestic automobile industry. Here's the kicker: The Japanese policymakers said they expected production to peak at *no more than 15,000 cars per year*. Today, with Honda, Nissan, Mitsubishi, and others as powerhouses of world industry, that number amounts to less than one day's production!

Had the United States insisted on truly free trade policies during those early postwar days, the fledgling democracies of German and Japan would have had no choice but to agree. Shortsightedly, we did not.

## Fairness *is* the Issue!

We helped nurture infant industries in Europe and Asia by welcoming their products to our shores. Some were considered junk. Few, if any, Japanese cars sold well in the United States during the forties, fifties, and early sixties. And though certain German products were considered to be of the highest quality—optical equipment, cutlery, chemicals, high-performance automobiles, and a few others—they made only a modest dent in world trade figures for many years.

By the 1980s, however, this was no longer the case. Foreign products, high in quality and competitively priced, began to flood U.S. markets: automobiles, steel, machine tools, semiconductors, airplanes. And though the inroads began in basic industries—industries, like steel, that our competitors had created as the basic building blocks of a strong economy—high-tech businesses were coming under increasing pressures as well.

My first significant efforts on the trade-policy front focused on getting U.S. workers and businesses fair or equal access to foreign markets. Beginning in 1985, shortly after I joined the Trade Subcommittee of the House Ways and Means Committee—an assignment I'd long desired—I became increasingly alarmed by our ballooning trade deficit. It was clear that the trade deficit wasn't simply a sign that people in other countries were making competitive products or goods we did not make ourselves. Rather, we were being systematically excluded from certain foreign markets. We were facing one-way free trade. The United States maintained the most open market in the world, whereas many of our trading partners were protecting their home markets.

In response, I outlined what I called a results-oriented trade policy, one that simply outlined what our negotiating priorities should be in the area of trade. Each year, countries with whom we had large and persistent trade deficits caused by a pattern of trade barriers would be singled out for consultations and negotiations in an effort to eliminate those barriers. If they refused to cooperate, we would demand a reduction in our bilateral trade deficit, leaving it up to that country to decide how to achieve it. They could increase their imports from the United States in any products they chose; they could limit their exports to the United States; or they could combine the two approaches. But if they failed to somehow address the unacceptable level of the trade barriers, penalties would be applied.

Soon after the legislation was introduced, the press and the business community began to assault it with a vengeance. Japan's and Europe's well-funded and skilled lobbyists went over to full-scale attack. Ultimately, Dan Rostenkowski and Lloyd Bentsen, two of the most distinguished members of Congress who'd originally promised to back the bill, got cold feet; they decided not to pursue the initiative.

So the initiative became known simply as the Gephardt Amendment. I refused to back down in the face of the lobbying that took place. Everywhere I went, I had to respond to challenges and attacks: "Are you a protectionist?" (Among laissez-faire economists, that was practically a dirty word.) "Are you against free trade?" "Are you trying to protect American workers and industries that are simply unable to compete?"

At the same time, and partly because of my efforts, the true extent and nature of trade barriers around the globe began to be uncovered. Privately, corporate leaders would tell me and my staff about problems they were facing in their efforts to penetrate overseas markets. They didn't want to be associated with me publicly for fear that other countries and business interests would retaliate against them. But, behind closed doors, they would tell me that they supported my efforts.

Some of the trade barriers American companies faced were simply ludicrous, and a few have passed into business folklore. For example, Japan refused to allow U.S. ski manufacturers to sell their products in that country because "Japanese snow was different"— and our skis had not been proven safe on Japanese slopes!

In another bizarre case, the Federal Express package-delivery company came to me for help. The Japanese government, they were sure, was delaying packages of U.S. origin as they passed through customs. But how? After some investigation, we found out. When packages were opened for inspection, a picture of the contents was made for the files. But cameras weren't used: In the land of Nikon and Minolta, the customs agency hired artists to craft pencil sketches of the contents!

Even Federal Express couldn't meet advertised delivery schedules with this kind of ridiculous delay. After I exposed the problem in the media, the Japanese came to the table within days to negotiate an end to the practice.

The passage of the Gephardt Amendment by the House sent shock waves throughout Washington and, I must say, around the world. Only later, when I visited a number of countries in Asia and was surprised to learn how much media and academic coverage my efforts had garnered, would I understand just how much international attention I'd received. During an Asia trip shortly after the 1988 election, I joked that my name was better known in Japan than it was in America!

The Gephardt Amendment was passed twice in the House of Representatives. The Senate, however, refused to take it up, preferring a somewhat more moderate bill known as Super 301. This proposal was designed to prioritize foreign barriers that future administrations would have to identify and seek to eliminate. It did make the administration accountable for identifying our trade priorities each year, but it provided too much flexibility, allowing administrations to avoid taking real action. Nevertheless, Super 301 was an improvement over prior law and became known as "Son of Gephardt." I still regret that Congress failed to approve the original model.

But I am pleased that today more Americans understand the unfair barriers American businesses face in global commerce. If we can get more and more people to understand the problems we can continue to press other countries in a united way to play fair.

We've made progress but we still have a long way to go. Our goal is to have world trade as free of barriers as trade is between the states of the United States.

# Fair Play and the Rights
# of American Workers

After the fight over market access and fair trade, I began an effort to broaden the trade agenda to make sure that trade would truly be a force for progress for all parties. At the heart of this equation is the issue of workers' rights and environmental concerns.

Workers' rights may sound like a topic mainly of interest to professional do-gooders or union spokespeople. But it is in the deep economic self-interest of every American to insist that other countries respect workers' rights. Let me explain why. We have heard through the media in recent years about how workers in some countries around the world are abused. We see pictures of Asian workers working in horrible conditions in "sweatshops" making garments and shoes for American consumers. Kathie Lee Gifford and Nike Shoes and others are criticized for not paying enough attention to the deplorable conditions of the workers producing clothes and athletic shoes for American consumption. Many instances of the use of child labor have been cited to the embarrassment of U.S. companies who scour the world looking for the cheapest possible labor costs.

Trade is supposed to help raise living standards. Unfortunately, in many developing countries around the world, workers and their families are paid subsistence wages at best. They are thankful when they get a job, and they have little power to demand higher pay and benefits. Companies are understandably always trying to find workers who will work for lower wages. But we Americans want opportunity to expand in all countries so that, over time, they will be peopled by millions of middle-class consumers who can buy both their own nations' products as well as imports from America. When that happens, trade is a true win-win situation. If workers in some nations are prevented from ever earning a living wage, they will never have enough money to consume goods and their countries will be successful producers but never active consumers. Consequently, the positive promise of global commerce for all people will never be achieved. As Henry Ford rightly pointed out, he needed to pay his workers a decent wage so that they could afford to buy the cars they were producing.

Furthermore, when wages increase in other countries, the downward pressure on U.S. wages is reduced. Relatively few things *must* be done here in the United States, other than for service jobs; most consumers don't really care whether the cars, clothes, stereos, and software they buy are made in Missouri, Mexico, or Malaysia. Thus, at some point a big wage differential between U.S. workers and foreign workers acts as an enticement for companies to move their operations elsewhere.

Clearly, much more than wages goes into a decision to relocate a plant. Companies consider the skills of the available workers, the political stability and laws of other countries, economic conditions, and many other factors. But wages play an increasing role in the decisions of companies that are locating plants.

So for our benefit as well as their own, workers should have a real opportunity to bargain for higher wages as they become more productive and as the quality of their work improves. Employees in developing nations won't immediately see their wages rise to the levels we enjoy here in the United States, but over time their standard of living should increase until it approaches ours. For similar reasons, workers' rights—including the right to bargain, the right to associate freely, and the right to strike—are all important. Unions can play a key role in defining and defending these rights, though they are not the only advocates workers have or need.

This link between the well-being of foreign workers and that of American employees is not theoretical or abstract. It's very real and concrete. It's been well documented that employers here in the United States use the threat—stated or implied—of moving their operations out of the country as a way to keep pay-increase requests to a minimum. During the debate on the North American Free Trade Agreement (NAFTA), for example, a surprising percentage of U.S. managers admitted that they intended to use the threat of moving to Mexico as a way to dampen wage demands. Ultimately, our wages are dependent on workers around the world earning a decent living. We are tied to them whether we like it or not.

The same threat has also been used to fight union organizing drives. Kate Bronfenbrenner, a professor at Cornell University, was commissioned to study this issue for the Department of Labor. When Kate came back with clear evidence of a majority of companies having used these threats to limit wage demands and union organizing activities, the department tried to bottle up the study. Later, it was forced to release its contents, but in the interim it gave the study to a group representing employers for review and response; in the meantime, it refused to defend Kate against their criticism. It was a sad episode in the history of U.S. labor policy.

Protection of the environment is another little-understood but vitally important trade issue. Of course, we Americans want all nations to help keep the world's air, water, and other natural resources clean and abundant, and trade agreements can provide some of the leverage we need to make that happen. But the environment is also an economic issue.

Here in the United States, we've been able—through years of debate and struggle—to pass relatively strict environmental regulations. We enjoy a more beautiful and healthful country as a result. The vast majority of Americans support these pro-environment rules, yet complying with them does come with a cost, part of which American businesses rightly bear. If American companies can move to other lands where environmental laws are unenforced or nonexistent, they will save money, helping the corporate bottom line (at least in the short run). Thus, the environment, like workers' rights, is a competitiveness issue. Moving the world toward shared environmental standards will benefit everybody's children and remove the incentives for companies to shop the world in search of pollution-friendly regimes.

As you can see, trade is much more than a matter of reducing tariffs between trading partners. It involves the competitive advantages each country has, the degree to which the rule of law operates to protect both businesses and working people, how labor markets operate, whether capital is protected, whether intellectual property—copyrights, patents, and trademarks—is respected, and a host of other interrelated issues.

In short, we must seek compatibility between countries so trade can be free and fair. Again, our goal must be, over the long-term, to get trade between all countries to be as fair, open, and compatible as it is between the states of the United States. I know we will not easily—or probably ever—have a common legal system, language, culture or currency. And, we should take pride in our national identities and diversity. But, we can make progress toward more compatibility in the trade arena.

Too many policymakers don't think trade rules matter to us or that it is too complicated to understand. Others are insulated from the results of their efforts. Policy mavens in Washington, in New York, and on university campuses sometimes talk casually about how trade policy inevitably produces "winners" and "losers." They fail to recognize that the "losers" have families and communities that rely on them. When bad policy decisions destroy U.S. jobs, neighborhoods and towns are often secondary victims. I don't consider these "acceptable casualties"—especially when we can do so much more to promote their interests.

A new, realistic approach to trade can minimize the number of losers and maximize the number of winners, and that must be our goal. But this demands a well-thought, long-term strategy—and that's what's been missing.

## The Battle Over NAFTA

In 1990, President Bush, responding to calls from Mexico's President Carlos Salinas, announced plans to begin negotiations with Canada and Mexico to expand the U.S.-Canada Free Trade Agreement to include Mexico in what would be called the North American Free Trade Agreement—NAFTA.

President Bush indicated that he wanted fast-track authority to negotiate trade agreements—fast track is so called because, under the approach Bush wanted, any agreement he reached would be guaranteed a vote in Congress (rather than being filibustered to death in the Senate, for example). A specific schedule for the consideration of trade agreements was to be included in fast-track authority.

But there's another key component of fast track: Congress cannot *amend* what the president submits; it can only vote "Yes" or "No." The goal is to minimize the involvement of members of Congress. Any representative with a specific trade-related concern is, therefore, put in the position of having to defeat the entire agreement to advance the interest he is advocating.

Early in 1991, I was the Majority Leader in Congress and was viewed as a key player on trade issues. Therefore, before President Bush formally requested fast-track authority from Congress, I sent him a long letter specifying elements I believed had to be in any negotiated agreement. I made it clear that if fast-track authority did not provide for these concerns, I would oppose his request and work in Congress to defeat it.

I'd spent a good amount of time studying Mexican laws regarding workers' rights and the environment. Although their laws weren't perfect—no country's are—they were actually quite advanced in a number of ways. Mexico's constitution, for example, included a family and medical leave provision years before we were able to pass a similar law under the Clinton administration.

The primary problem was the lack of enforcement of the laws. Unless citizens have the power and government officials have the resources to ensure that laws are enforced, the best legislation in the world means little. I saw NAFTA as potentially giving us the ability to promote enforcement of the laws in Mexico, which would be of enormous economic benefit to us as well as promoting the health and safety of those who lived along the U.S.-Mexico border. I saw NAFTA as a possible force for progress that could work to get Mexico to actually enforce its own worker and environmental standards so more compatibility could be achieved between the U.S. and Mexico and trade could benefit both countries. This was a major part of the plan I presented to the Bush administration.

As the NAFTA talks began, I traveled to Mexico to meet with President Salinas. He was a charismatic figure who spent a great deal of time during our meeting explaining how his "Solidarity" program was bringing electricity, water, education, and health care to poor communities across his nation. I liked what I heard, but I stressed my goals for the negotiations, wanting to make it clear that NAFTA would pass only if proper protections for U.S. interests were included.

I also traveled, unannounced, to the U.S.-Mexico border region. There, trade, labor, and environmental issues all come together in a very visible way. On the Mexican side of the line there were clustered thousands of *maquiladoras*—factories whose primary purpose is to make products for export to the United States. A half-million or more poor Mexicans worked in these plants, many for pennies an hour, often manufacturing products previously made in the United States. Because of the poverty in Mexico, these workers had little bargaining power. Employers colluded to set wages, and if any employees protested or sought to organize their fellow workers they were blacklisted—or worse.

I made five visits to the U.S.-Mexico border, flying to cities on the U.S. side and driving across. Each time, I was accompanied by dedicated organizers like Ed Feighan and Victor Muñoz, who took the time to meet with local community leaders and citizens and researched the local economy in preparation for my visits. I was also joined on many of my trips by Harley Shaiken, a university professor who is an expert on Latin American affairs and industrial relations; for me and many other members of Congress he was one of our most valuable resources—as well as a personal friend. Mark Anderson, another close friend and adviser, also joined us on several trips. Otherwise, we worked hard to keep my visits hush-hush. I feared that if people knew I was coming the government and the employers would coerce people into changing their stories.

Indeed, during one visit with several other members of Congress and a crew from CNN we were confronted by company guards. They were upset that we had seen the barracks where up to 600 high school–aged kids—workers for U.S. companies located on the border—were jammed together in bunk beds. CNN's camera crew was surrounded by guards and asked to turn over their videotape. Luckily, they'd hidden the real tape just before the guards got there; the tape they surrendered was blank.

Some of the factories we saw in Mexico were as modern and well equipped as you'll find anywhere in the world. But the nearby communities where the Mexican workers live are another story. Many actually use the packing materials and the cardboard boxes that carry the products they make to the United States to build their shacks. Many communities have no running water and no sanitary facilities; raw sewage usually runs in a ditch a few feet from where children play. Some workers literally live in worse conditions than some domestic animals endure in America. My visits to these communities profoundly affected me and my views about trade. I came away with a burning desire to improve conditions for Mexican and American workers alike.

The environmental degradation around the factories is extraordinary. At the site of a former battery recycling plant we saw small hills containing thousands of metric tons of battery waste that were leeching into the ground—next to a dairy farm. Children in the area—those that could actually afford it—drank the milk from these contaminated cows. Mexico boasts strong labor and environmental laws—stronger than ours, in some cases—but few are adequately enforced.

We visited some schools, which were attended by few of the village children; many could not afford clothes, books, or even pencils. At one school, the mothers followed me out to the car and begged me to go to the owners of the plants to ask them to give some supplies to the school.

During one visit, our van was tailed by police seeking to intimidate us. At one point, they switched on their red lights, demanding that we pull over. Luckily, we had arranged for security on this trip, having learned how the local police operated. They forced the local police to back down. But our efforts to visit factories—factories owned by U.S. companies, mind you—were met with refusal after refusal. I'm told that local employers operate a telephone chain that alerts all the companies about outside investigators in a matter of minutes, so that visitors like me are effectively locked out.

All this existed before NAFTA. It was my hope that a strong trade agreement that provided the necessary resources to clean up the border and protect human health and safety could begin to reverse the devastation I saw.

But the AFL-CIO and many of its member unions were upset with my position. They flatly opposed NAFTA and wanted me to have nothing to do with it. But I could not walk away from being intimately involved in the negotiations. It would largely be up to me to define whether or not an agreement met the crucial standards we'd defined.

## The Games Behind the Treaty

In early 1992, while President Bush was trying to bring the NAFTA negotiations to a close, it became clear that Bill Clinton was going to win the Democratic nomination for president. In addition to our casual friendship, I had several personal ties to Bill Clinton. My former aide, George Stephanopolous, had become one of his chief advisers, and Paul Begala, as well as other former aides and friends, were signing up to join the Clinton campaign.

I wanted to help elect Bill Clinton, not only because he was a Democrat but also because he wanted to fight for health care reform, a cleaner environment, and a host of other causes I shared. On balance, these positives outweighed my concerns over NAFTA—especially since Clinton had vowed to improve the agreement.

In the end, I agreed to work closely with Clinton and his campaign staff to craft the speech he delivered in North Carolina announcing his support for NAFTA coupled with his determination to modify and strengthen the deal Bush had cut.

Fast-forward now to August 1993, eight months into President Clinton's first term in office. The NAFTA negotiations were finally coming to a close. On Sunday night, my staff was given the final text of the proposed "side agreements" covering labor and the environment. They worked into the night with the U.S. negotiators, reviewing the document line by line.

On Monday, I came into the office, ready to meet with my staff to determine whether or not I would be able to support the final agreement. They asked me to read the agreement in its entirety first. The issue was simply too important for my views to be colored by other people's impressions and calculations. This should and would be my decision—based not on political advice but on the concrete terms of the treaty, its strengths and its weaknesses.

I finished reading the agreement and called the staff into my office. Expecting a long discussion, they had come armed with legal data, alternative negotiating texts, and other documents. Instead, I shook my head and simply said, "I can't support NAFTA. It doesn't meet the goals I set out, and it won't make things better. I have to say, 'No.'"

The agreement lacked teeth in allowing either country to get the other country to actually enforce their labor and environmental laws. The negotiators argued that "side agreements" gave the ability of either side to get the other side to properly enforce their laws, but it was obvious the side agreements were on the "side" because the Mexican government didn't want us to have the ability to stop trade if they didn't enforce their laws. The side agreements were a hoax.

To get NAFTA ratified by Congress, a massive lobbying campaign was mounted on its behalf by the administration; millions of dollars were spent by the business community. The White House created a "war room" modeled after Clinton's 1992 presidential campaign headquarters, where the best staff they could find were gathered to lobby for the president's position. Every member's vote was tallied; many were called four, five, or more times.

The president, the vice president, and the cabinet got personally involved in the lobbying effort. Deals of every kind were offered. Some members were promised special arrangements favorable to citrus and tomato farmers in their districts; even the corn broom manufacturers got into the game—along with many others. Members were promised bridges, roads, and other projects. The administration's efforts on behalf of NAFTA ended up looking more like a broadcast of "Let's Make a Deal" than a serious debate on a major national policy.

## The Tragedy of NAFTA

The day NAFTA passed was one of my darkest in Congress. I believe I spent more time grappling with NAFTA and the underlying issues than had any other person. To me, it was clear that the treaty was flawed and would endanger our standard of living—not just in obvious, immediate ways but gradually, by changing the competitive structure under which we deal with other countries.

The agreements affecting labor and environmental issues are sadly inadequate. They lack teeth—the ability to coerce another country to enforce its own laws. And for political reasons they are seldom even mentioned; instead, most problems are simply swept under the rug. Of course, the proponents of NAFTA have a great deal invested, politically speaking, in rubber-stamping Mexico's policies, even when they are misguided.

In the five years since NAFTA passed, the number of plants and workers in Mexico on our border has doubled. In 1993, there were 500,000 workers on the border—now there are one million. Mexican workers earn less now than they did five years ago and living conditions have obviously worsened. In my two trips to the border since NAFTA, I really believe things have gotten worse—not better. It is obvious that more trade with Mexico will not change conditions that are dictated by their government policies.

Also, the additional trade with Mexico caused by NAFTA has not benefitted American businesses or workers. Whereas, we had a positive trade balance with Mexico before NAFTA—now we have a deficit. It's no wonder—most of our exports to Mexico are "industrial tourists"—parts that go to Mexico to be put into finished products to be shipped back to the U.S. for consumption here. Of course, Mexican workers have even less income to buy any products—made in Mexico or wherever. NAFTA's only accomplishment is to give the United States and other global businesses easier access to low-cost Mexican labor, which helps with profits but little of that lower cost goes to U.S. consumers. Worse than anything, because we missed the opportunity to use NAFTA to get laws better enforced in Mexico we missed the chance to build, over time, a huge number of middle-class consumers in Mexico. What the world needs now is more able consumers—not just more able producers.

# Trade and the Values We Cherish

In 1989, the leaders of China quelled a rebellion of students in Tiananmen Square in Beijing with deadly force. Millions of people all around the globe will never forget the televised image of that man single-handedly staring down a tank. He is a lasting symbol of the confrontation between the power of violence and the power of an idea and will be remembered long after the purveyors of violence are no more.

How and why does the battle for human rights in China affect us? Once again, economics—specifically, international trade—provides a focal point.

*Most-favored-nation status*—commonly known by the acronym MFN—is a term of art from the field of global trade. A country granted this status by the United States will enjoy lower tariffs and trade barriers than those countries without it. Clearly, it's a powerful economic tool that we must use intelligently to promote American interests around the world.

Our trade relations with China have some similarities to what we face with Mexico. But in China's case the differences with the U.S. are even greater. Mexico has good laws on human rights and worker rights that are not well enough enforced. China has few such laws and is one of the most repressive regimes on earth in terms of human and labor rights. Chinese citizens are routinely arrested and imprisoned for simply uttering political statements calling for freedom or expressing criticism of the government. Chinese prisoners are made to manufacture products for sale in global commerce—with absolutely no compensation. It is difficult to see how much of China's exports to us can be seen as "fair" trade. And the idea that more trade with China is by itself bringing about political and cultural change in China is ludicrous.

Since 1989, I have fought to persuade first President Bush, then President Clinton, to respond aggressively to China's failure to grant its people the most basic internationally recognized human rights. Each year we've debated the issue forcefully, and each year we've lost the vote in Congress to overturn the presidential waiver of sanctions against China.

Advocates of MFN status for China say that we can't cut ourselves out of the largest market in the world—a country with 1.2

billion people. They oppose tariffs on Chinese products because these products are increasingly important to our own consumers. And, they say, if we don't do business with China, other countries will gladly pick up the slack.

All of that may be true. But America has to stand for something more than money. Our economic policies must be undergirded by values—democracy and freedom chief among them.

Unlike most societies, the United States did not simply evolve out of a shared culture, language, or geography. America is a nation conceived in principle, and that principle is human liberty. It began with a simple sentence that is still the most revolutionary statement ever put on paper: "We hold these truths to be self-evident: that all men are created equal, that they are endowed by their creator with certain unalienable rights, that among these are Life, Liberty, and the pursuit of Happiness."

The Founders of our nation never intended those words to apply to only a few million people living in thirteen colonies on the eastern shore of North America. Just a few weeks before his death, fifty years to the day from the signing of the Declaration of Independence, Thomas Jefferson wrote of that document, "May it be to the world, what I believe it will be (to some parts sooner, to others later, but finally to all), the signal of arousing men to burst their chains."

One of the great heroes of China's democracy movement is a former electrician named Wei Jingsheng. In 1978, Wei displayed a poster on a brick wall in Xidan. On it he wrote, "The results of all struggle involving the people's resistance to oppression and exploitation are determined by their success or failure in obtaining democracy!" For sentiments like these, he was arrested, convicted, and sentenced to fifteen years in prison. He languished there until

September of 1993, when he was released six months early, just as China was mounting an all-out campaign to win the right to host the 2000 Summer Olympic Games.

In 1995, a year in which he was nominated for the Nobel Peace Prize, Wei was formally charged with attempting to overthrow the Chinese government. In his defense statement he spoke in the universal language of the Declaration of Independence, calling freedom of speech, freedom of the press, freedom of assembly, and the right of appeal to the government "inalienable rights belonging to the people, the masters of the country." After a six-hour trial, he was sentenced to prison for fourteen more years. He was kept in an unheated cell with bright lights glaring twenty-four hours a day.

In a letter written from his prison cell to Chinese leaders, Wei said that human rights "are common objective standards which apply to all governments and all individuals. . . . Like objective existence and objective laws, they are objective truths. That was why Rousseau called them 'natural rights.'"

Wei is right: Basic human rights are universal aspirations, not a cultural preference.

In 1997, Wei was released from prison on "medical parole" and sent into exile to the United States. Shortly after his arrival here, I had the opportunity to meet him. It was a meeting I will never forget. Wei is a hero of mine.

Wei thanked me and other members of Congress for our efforts to secure his release. Because of us, he said, China's leaders were held accountable; it was the annual MFN debate in Congress that had helped to keep him and other political prisoners alive. But with sadness in his voice Wei told me, "In truth, I am not yet free. I cannot return to China because if I did I would be arrested as a criminal. Until I can go home, I remain a prisoner."

The rule of law is a precondition not just to democracy and human rights but also to economic justice, stability, and freedom. If human rights can be trampled upon, so can the rights of businesses who want and expect their interests to be protected. A country that has no qualms about imprisoning political dissidents will also feel free to seize the assets of foreign companies, crush competition, and ride roughshod over property rights. It's no accident that capitalism first took root in the countries of Western Europe and North America with the strongest traditions of political liberty: The two go hand in hand.

That's the economic rationale for supporting human rights around the world—a cause that, in any case, is simply the right thing to fight for.

## The Ongoing Debate

Since the debate over NAFTA and our trade relations with China, the biggest trade issue has been whether or not to give President Clinton the authority to negotiate further free trade treaties (like NAFTA) with other countries. I've opposed these efforts because I want to be sure we cure the defects we still have in NAFTA—in new free trade treaties.

In late 1996, in anticipation of a push on fast track by the Clinton administration, I directed my staff to meet with senior White House officials. The political lessons I'd learned from the NAFTA maneuvering weren't lost on me. We let the administration know that we hoped to find common ground. But I wouldn't simply bide my time while we talked. While they were out organizing, I would be, too.

In the fall of 1997, the administration pressed forward on a fast-track proposal, supported by some Democrats and many Republicans. The administration refused to say what they wanted to negotiate—rather, they argued that Clinton deserved the authority because his predecessors had been given it. That's not a good enough reason. This proposal didn't guarantee that worker and environmental laws would have to be enforced. In fact, their proposal *prohibited* real progress on worker and environmental provisions in future free trade treaties. It didn't move us in the right direction—it moved us in the wrong direction. House Speaker Newt Gingrich was forced to pull the bill because the votes simply weren't there. Too many constituents were telling their representatives that a new approach was needed.

I prepared an alternative approach. It would have guaranteed the president a vote on an agreement if he fulfilled the objectives that Congress outlined. We also would have placed workers' rights and environmental issues on a par with issues like intellectual property and investment protections. My approach did not seek to impose U.S. law—for example, the U.S. minimum wage, or occupational health and safety laws—upon other countries. Yet other countries must enforce their existing laws and international commitments in these two areas.

In the end, the Republican approach failed to pass Congress. In 1998, the Republicans once again tried to push their fast-track approach, perhaps hoping to divide Democrats and to divert the attention of organized labor just before the midterm elections. In a major defeat, seventy-one Republicans deserted their leadership and voted with the vast majority of Democrats to defeat fast track.

The trade debate is not over. Far from it. We've succeeded in expanding the agenda but not yet in making human rights, workers' rights, and environmental protection into permanent, central elements of the American negotiating position. Only when we do so can we hope to craft a trade strategy effectively dedicated to promoting a high and rising standard of living around the globe as well as the universal ideals of life, liberty, and the pursuit of happiness.

Some people ask: If we can improve our productivity through more collaboration among workers and employers and through better education and training, why do we need to worry about fair trade? The question reflects the assumption made by many experts that *any* trade, fair or unfair, is ultimately good for everyone.

This kind of thinking surprises me. Of course, we need to boost our national productivity; it's a topic to which much of this book is devoted. But we also need to demand a level playing field for our businesses and workers. It won't be easy to achieve, but we owe it to ourselves to try.

If the new global economy is to work for everyone's benefit and a brighter future for all, we must lead the effort to make all trade as fair and compatible as it can possibly be.

When citizens speak out to their representatives and public servants as they did in the NAFTA debate and the China MFN debate—we make progress in leading the world toward fair trade. While its very important to educate our people and run our businesses so our workers are motivated and productive—it is equally important to get global trade to be fair. For this to happen—just as we need, as citizens, to take ownership of our educational and business institutions—we need to take ownership of our trade institutions to insist on fairness in global commerce.

# II

# Our Families,
# Our Future

SOLUTIONS FOR THE "QUIET CRISIS"

# "How Can God Let This Happen?"

Sometimes, it takes a crisis to make you fully appreciate the value of what you have—and how easily it can be lost. For our family, my son Matt's struggle with cancer was such a crisis.

In May 1972, my wife Jane brought eighteen-month-old Matt to Children's Hospital in St. Louis. For about two weeks, he'd been having flu symptoms that he couldn't seem to shake, so his pediatrician recommended that she bring Matt to the hospital for an X-ray exam. It all sounded pretty routine. But at about eleven o'clock in the morning, Jane called me at the law office where I worked. Between sobs, she told me to come to the hospital immediately—something was horribly wrong with Matt.

I'll never forget walking into the hospital and meeting Jane, accompanied by an unfamiliar doctor, at the front door. The doctor was an oncologist—a cancer specialist—named Theresa Vietti. In her office, Dr. Vietti broke the news. Matt had a cancerous growth the size of a volleyball on his prostate gland. She explained that this type of tumor—technically known as a rhabdomyosarcoma—was usually seen behind the eye. The location of Matt's tumor was very rare; only one or two other cases like his had been reported in the United States.

Matt's prognosis was grim. The tumor was very aggressive; in Dr. Vietti's experience, this type of cancer usually spread, or metastasized, very quickly, and she thought that this would likely happen in Matt's case. The tumor was already so large that it was closing down Matt's capacity to eliminate waste. Dr. Vietti flatly predicted that Matt would live only a few more weeks.

Horrified, Jane and I asked, "Isn't there anything you can do?"

Dr. Vietti was doubtful. The tumor, she explained, was too large to remove surgically. She and the other doctors would investigate the possibility of chemotherapy, but she had little confidence in their ability to affect such a large cancerous mass.

Jane and I were devastated. Numb with shock and terror, we drove home to get supplies and clothes for Matt's hospitalization—as we thought, for the final days of his life. Later that afternoon, the emotions overwhelmed us. Helpless tears streamed down our faces. All I could think was, "How can God let this happen to a beautiful eighteen-month-old child—a child so young that we can't even tell him why he is in such pain?"

At home that night, Jane and I knelt beside our bed and prayed all night that Matt might be saved—that somehow he might live. It was the first of many such sleepless nights of prayer. I almost believed that if we prayed earnestly enough and often enough, God would save our son.

Early the next morning, back at the hospital, we received our first glimmer of hope. A young resident, Dr. Abdel Ragab, told us about some computer research he'd done into Matt's case during the night. He'd discovered that this kind of tumor was being treated with a special triple-drug chemotherapy at St. Jude's Children's Research Hospital in Memphis, founded by the late entertainer Danny Thomas, and at M. D. Anderson Hospital in Houston. The results were fairly good when the tumor was located behind the eye, but Dr. Ragab cautioned us that it might not work in Matt's case. Nonetheless, he thought that triple-drug therapy, in conjunction with massive radiation treatments, might shrink the tumor, that it was worth a try.

Dr. Vietti was less sanguine. She urged us to consider whether we really wanted to put Matt through the pain that this experimental therapy would cause. "All of this work will probably not save him," she cautioned. "And even if it does, Matt will be left with lots of collateral problems that may be so severe his life after cancer could be a very unhappy one. Maybe it would be better to spare him the pain of the therapy in pursuit of such a questionable result."

Of course, the decision would be ours. The doctors wouldn't start the chemotherapy until the next day.

Again, Jane and I prayed all night. We came to the conclusion that we had to try to save Matt's life. We were convinced that, even if Matt suffered considerable physical damage, we could somehow give him enough of a positive mental attitude to make a happy life possible. The next morning, we were at the hospital bright and early to give the go-ahead on chemotherapy.

Yet even before the therapy could begin we were faced with a new problem. Matt had contracted pneumonia, and the chemotherapy could not start until the infection was licked. The next week was the most frightening part of the entire experience. Matt was in intense pain because he could barely urinate; all of his body systems were shutting down because of the tumor. Jane and I felt helpless; we couldn't even talk to Matt to explain what was happening. All we could do was hope and pray that the antibiotics would eliminate the pneumonia so we could start the chemotherapy that might—just might—shrink the tumor. Jane and I took turns keeping vigil at the hospital, battling alongside the doctors and nurses for Matt's life.

One night, we were trying to get Matt to sleep through the night so he could build up strength to fight the infection. The problem was that the doctors and nurses kept barging into the room and waking him up for tests and medications. Thoroughly exasperated, I finally stationed my chair outside Matt's room and physically barred the nurses and doctors so he could get four hours of rest. (I had to tell one resident, "You'll get into the room to take Matt's blood pressure over my dead body." Believe me, he did *not* get in.)

A few days later, the pneumonia went away, and we were able to start the chemotherapy.

## The Lucky Ones

After a week-long course of therapy, the tumor had been reduced enough so that Matt could urinate again. It meant we could take him home. I thanked God for this sign of progress— such a small sign, yet such a big one—for we'd thought that Matt would never leave the hospital alive.

We brought Matt back to the hospital periodically for further chemotherapy treatments, often for an overnight stay so he could get "drip therapy" through an intravenous tube. Often I would sit and talk with the parents of other children getting similar cancer treatments. Drawn together by our common ordeal, we poured out our fears and troubles to one another.

Many of the parents I talked to had no health insurance or had insurance that did not cover their child's illness. They had to pay the $300 for each chemotherapy treatment in cash. Some said they had to borrow or beg for the money from friends, relatives, and neighbors. One father told me that he was living in terror—not just because he thought his son might die but also because he feared he couldn't afford the next chemotherapy treatment. Jane and I were two of the lucky ones—I had a good job, a supportive employer, and a strong health insurance policy. Many others aren't so lucky.

We and some of the other parents who had insurance decided to set up a fund to help pay for treatments for uninsured families. To raise money, we collected used books from neighbors and friends for a big sale each fall. This was therapeutic in more ways than one: Working on the book fairs allowed us to help others while keeping us busy and distracting us from our fears.

About a month after Matt's chemotherapy and radiation treatments had begun, Jane again called me at the office in tears. But this time they were tears of joy. After Matt's afternoon nap, she had felt his stomach. It had been as hard as a rock from the tumor, but now it was soft—the tumor had shrunk dramatically. Ecstatic, Jane told me that she'd been praying while Matt slept that the tumor would recede, and as she prayed she'd felt a warm feeling envelop her. Clearly, God's love was at work in all of our lives.

Over the next three years, Matt faced additional courses of chemotherapy and radiation. He suffered it all willingly and without complaints, even making brave jokes about feeling sick and about losing his hair.

By the end of that first summer, the doctors reported that Matt's tumor was too small to see on an X-ray. They recommended an operation to try to remove whatever was left. They had no idea what they would find, but they would take out anything affected by the tumor.

Before Matt's operation, Jane and I wanted to get him away from St. Louis, the hospital, and all the pain he'd experienced. I asked his doctor if we could take him away for a week's vacation. The doctor reluctantly agreed, and we rented a cabin on a sparsely populated island off the northern tip of the Door Peninsula in Wisconsin.

I remember vividly how wonderful that week was. Jane and I would lay Matt down for a nap and sit next to his bed and watch him sleep, deeply happy that we were with him and that he was alive—though we couldn't know for how long. Life, we realized, is so precious. I'll never take it for granted again.

Dr. Jessie Ternberg had predicted that Matt's surgery would take two or three hours. It actually took four hours, and we were increasingly tense and afraid, imagining the worse. When Dr. Ternberg finally came into the waiting room, I remember the afternoon sunlight streaming through the window—a sign, I felt, that God was smiling on us. But the news was troubling. Dr. Ternberg had taken out Matt's prostate gland and his bladder because both had been so involved with the tumor.

Jane and I winced. We knew this was a big problem. But we'd gotten through darker times than this. We hugged, and I told Jane, "It could have been much worse. The doctor says she got all the cancer and that Matt's prognosis is good. We can deal with the problems—we can make this work!"

As Matt grew up, I worried that he would feel bad because he had suffered so much physical damage. Jane and I made a special effort always to remind him that he was the luckiest person in the world. I think I most often asked God, besides letting Matt live, to help him feel glad to be alive and never to feel sorry for himself. God has surely granted this prayer. To this day, Matt has an extremely positive, optimistic outlook that makes him a joy to all who know him.

Matt has had some seven additional operations to repair the collateral damage caused by his therapy. In 1981, the original operation deteriorated because of problems associated with the radiation treatment. The necessary surgery was very complicated. The only surgeon who could really handle it, we were told, was Dr. Hardy Hendren in Boston.

We flew there to see Dr. Hendren. After studying X-rays and examining Matt, he said he could fix both problems in a single, but complicated, procedure. In August 1981, Matt had a thirteen-hour operation that accomplished both goals.

The day after the operation, Dr. Hendren explained that Matt would be woozy all day. To keep me busy, the doctor invited me to scrub up and accompany him in the operating room. It was one of the most memorable days of my life. Dr. Hendren started operating at six o'clock in the morning and kept going till midnight. He had two residents who opened and closed patients for him in separate operating rooms; Dr. Hendren would then go in to do the hard part. I was in awe at his focus, concentration, and discipline. He was able to close out the entire world for eighteen hours straight and withstand the pressures of dealing with human life every minute.

Today, as I mentioned earlier, Matt is a twenty-eight-year-old aspiring entrepreneur, a recent business school graduate in the throes of launching a new venture in sports marketing. Matt married a wonderful young woman, Trisha Tholen, in 1998. When Jane and I walked him down the aisle there were tears of joy and thanks in our eyes. To look at him, you'd never know how close he came to leaving this earth forever. But he lives every day, I think, with the extra zest that comes from knowing what a wonderful gift life really is.

A health crisis is one of the gravest tests any family can face. It often causes fights and acrimony; in some cases it results in divorce. Thankfully, I'm married to an extraordinary woman. Jane's strength in handling Matt's illness was nothing short of amazing. I've always loved and admired her level, low-key attitude toward trouble, and during this crisis it was perhaps literally lifesaving. She never lost her cool or got pessimistic, and she was a wonderful nurse for all of Matt's physical problems. Most important, his positive attitude was more a product of Jane's constant encouragement than anything else. She could not have been better for him than she was. I thank God for Jane. She has been a steady, loving partner over thirty-two years. I'm a very lucky person to have found her.

Matt's illness taught me to appreciate the little things that we so often take for granted; it made me humble, grateful, and very happy to just be near my family, living our daily lives. Today, I find I'm never really distraught over political setbacks, money worries, or other troubles; as long as my family is healthy, I have everything I need. Matt's illness changed my life more deeply than anything else I've experienced—for the better.

# First Comes Health

As my family's experience with Matt taught us, a family coping with health problems can't focus on anything else. Your life is placed on hold when illness strikes. For many families who lack access to good health care, and who often have to cope with chronic health conditions exacerbated by stress and poverty, it's a problem that makes career, education, and other aspirations seem like impossible dreams rather than a natural part of life.

For the past ten years, Jane has worked as an administrator for a group of pediatricians in northern Virginia. She sees on a daily basis the myriad problems families have getting adequate health care—and most of her patients have health insurance!

Jane also serves on the board of directors of the Children's Inn at the National Institutes of Health (NIH). Children's Inn houses families of gravely or terminally ill children who come for treatment at the NIH from all over the world. She has met many children with life-threatening illnesses who have little or no health coverage.

Our own family experiences and Jane's observations have convinced me that we must strive to improve the American system for delivering health care. There's no question that we have the best doctors, nurses, hospitals, and medical technology in the world. But we can do a much better job of making sure that every family in need of health care gets it.

Our most pressing challenge is to provide some kind of health insurance coverage for the roughly 40 million Americans without it. This was the primary focus of President Clinton's 1993 health care initiative, which we failed to enact. That proposal would have required all businesses to provide coverage for every employee. The idea was very unpopular among small-business owners, and that unpopularity was probably one of the reasons the plan failed.

Since then, I've thought a lot about how to solve the problem. Back in 1993, we rejected the idea of raising federal taxes to provide health insurance for anyone not covered through an employer, and I think we were right to do so. However, we did subsequently pass an initiative to provide states with federal money to help cover more children, and in many states it's making a significant difference. I suspect most small-business owners would like to cover their employees but find it hard to foot the bills. A tax incentive might make the difference. Many of today's uninsured are employed in small businesses, so this approach is a promising one.

The other troublesome problem in health care today concerns the quality of "managed care," a rapidly growing type of insurance plan. During the early- and mid-1990s, health providers were pressed hard by consumers and businesses alike to find ways to slow the growth of health care costs. This pressure both provoked the Clinton initiative and was heightened by it. Critics, however, argued that if Clinton plan passed the quality of American health care would decline as millions were herded into managed-care programs, where decisions about their own treatment would be taken from them. Ironically, this is precisely what happened—but without the Clinton plan. Instead, pressure to join managed-care plans came mainly from employers worried about the costs of employee-benefit programs. Managed care reduces medical expenses by setting up gatekeepers who must approve treatment before it is given and by establishing protocols that limit the number of doctor visits, days in the hospital, and kinds of tests that can be paid for in connection with a particular diagnosis. Insurance costs are

Matt, Jane, Dick, Kate, and Chrissy Gephardt in 1980

The Gephardt family today: Marc Leibole and wife Chrissy; Trisha and Matt Gephardt; Dick and Jane Gephardt; Jason Schenk and Kate Gephardt

Sharing a Christmas wish
with Santa, 1945

The boyhood home in St. Louis
at 6263 River Place

"Mayor for a day" in St. Louis, 1956

Our wedding day,
August 13, 1966

My parents, Loreen and Lou,
with me and my brother,
Don, behind

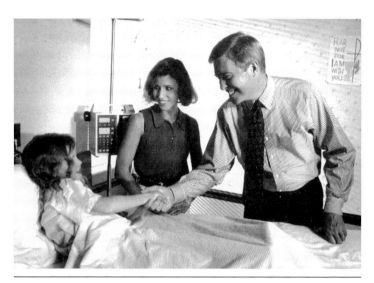

Visiting families at a St. Louis-area hospital

The young congressman visiting St. Louis area schools

Learning about a reading program from junior high students
(that's Mike Wessel over my right shoulder)

Pitching in at a neighborhood cleanup

Greeting factory workers

Visiting a St. Louis-area business

Meeting with the Machinists union members at
McDonnell Douglas in St. Louis

Explaining health care reform options at St. Louis Town Hall

Addressing the Democratic Convention, Chicago, 1996

no longer growing as fast as they were during the early 1990s, yet millions of Americans are now complaining that health care decisions have been taken away from them and their physicians and turned over to insurance-company bureaucrats who care only about profits.

Recently, Congress considered a so-called Patient's Bill of Rights. The proposed legislation would guarantee such basic rights as the right to get emergency hospital care and the right to independent arbitration over the advisability of particular medical procedures. One of its most controversial features would have made health maintenance organizations (HMOs) subject to malpractice suits, as physicians have always been. Because HMOs are making crucial decisions about the medical procedures a patient receives, the idea is that HMOs should be held legally liable for the consequences of those decisions. The insurance companies, of course, are opposed.

I support the Patient's Bill of Rights. I think it's a reasonable step toward protecting consumers from the excesses of today's increasingly market-driven, profit-oriented health care companies. Having said that, I must stress that quality health care will never be provided as a result of government action alone. Individual citizens also have an important responsibility to take care of their health and to investigate, analyze, and monitor their health care plans before and after enrolling. Uncle Sam can make it easier by gathering and disclosing more information and data about consumer experience with various health plans. We already do that for federal employees; we should be able to do it for all Americans.

The federal government also has an important role in supporting basic health research at the National Institutes of Health. The roughly $13 billion we spend on that research annually is a prime reason our health care is the best in the world. Right now, at century's end, we're on the brink of dramatic new breakthroughs because of the Human Genome Project, which is mapping every gene that determines our individual biological inheritance, including our varied susceptibility to heart disease, cancer, and countless other diseases. This research holds out the promise that within a few years we'll understand the root causes of many of humankind's greatest historic enemies and be able to develop new and more effective strategies for combating them.

These benefits are the direct result of federal support for medical research. The cost is small—about $50 dollars per year for each American citizen. The potential return is incalculable. How dare some of my Republican colleagues claim—with a straight face—that government is the enemy?

## A Community to Lean On

Painful as Matt's health crisis was, our family was able to weather it because of the great support system we had in place—not only in the form of access to medical care but also in family, friends, and a community of neighbors who cared, prayed, and helped in ways large and small. Millions of Americans aren't so lucky; many face similar crises each year without adequate help. A mission I take very seriously in my role as a political leader is the responsibility to do something about this—to give all Americans access to the help their families need to stay together and to care for one another in good times and bad. That is why I fought so hard for health care reform in 1993—to give people access to health care—and I will never quit fighting for a patient's bill of rights.

Once you fight a grave illness like Matt's you are forever changed. You never forget the terror and you never lose the commitment to fight for families who are fighting for their lives.

Furthermore, this is not just a matter of help during times of catastrophe. Social support for families is a lifetime issue. Human needs begin at birth—even in the womb—and how fully they are met can affect the well-being of families and individuals for a life-time.

Recently, I visited Boston Medical Center and met Dr. Barry Zuckerman, one of our nation's leading pediatricians. He told me about the programs he and his colleagues have established there to help children and families from one of Boston's poorest neigh-borhoods get a high-quality start in life. His work is a shining ex-ample of how neighborhood institutions—in this case a health clinic—can play a pivotal role in helping families do what they of-ten can't do alone.

Of course, the first responsibility borne by Barry and the doc-tors, nurses, and other professionals at the hospital is for the phys-ical well-being of the children they see—and the medical care they dispense is of world-class quality. Yet early during his career at the hospital Barry realized that psychological, emotional, social, and economic factors were profoundly impacting the health of his pa-tients. Gradually, he began expanding the clinic's offerings to ad-dress some of these larger needs.

One of the first things Barry did was hire a legal-aid lawyer to work with parents and children at the clinic. "I got fed up with treating kids who were suffering from ear infections, serious colds, asthma, and other ailments that were made worse by fixable social problems," he points out. "These kids belonged to families that were getting evicted, having the heat in their apartments turned off, and having their food stamps cut off—often unfairly. I knew that if we could help these people get the assistance they were legally and morally entitled to, their health problems would quickly improve."

The program proved to be so popular and effective that today the clinic employs three legal-aid lawyers, each of whom works for a relative pittance—half the salary of a social worker. In addition to counseling patients and families, they train the doctors at the clinics to recognize and assist with legal issues as they arise.

To provide families with additional help in coping with complicated bureaucracies, the clinic provides space for a desk manned by student volunteers from nearby Harvard University. These volunteers track information about the activities of community organizations and government offices in order to advise parents about whom to call when problems arise, say, with the local welfare department, a school official, or a landlord. "Most of our client families have no idea that they can pick up a phone and call their congressman or state legislator for help," Barry explains. "Our volunteers show them how to do this, and they'll even sit with a parent and help them make the call. This is how real-life problems get solved."

The hospital goes to unusual lengths to educate parents about what they can do to help their children grow up healthy, happy, and smart. The hospital's program known as Reach Out and Read is an example. Ten years ago, Barry and his colleagues had gotten into the habit of bringing children's books into the clinic waiting room to entertain kids and parents while they waited for an appointment. One day, one of the doctors complained, "You know, some of our families are walking away with those books." A lightbulb turned on. "Maybe that's *not* a bad thing," Barry commented, and Reach Out and Read was born. Today, donors regularly provide age-appropriate children's books—from the Dr. Seuss classics to *Goodnight Moon*—to be given free to clinic patients and their parents. More important, every pediatrician at the clinic is trained to give out the books and to take time to explain to parents the importance and benefits of reading with their child for twenty minutes each day. "The impact of having a doctor saying this is so much greater than if the families just helped themselves to a book on their way out the door," Barry explains.

Reach Out and Read plays a critical role in helping new parents interact with their child in a way that pays huge dividends later in life. Barry explains, "When a six-month-old sees her parent open a book to read to her, she usually smiles. When Mom smiles back, a powerful connection is created not only between parent and child but between the intellectual and emotional parts of the child's brain. Suddenly, books and learning become pleasurable. The child grows up with a love of reading that will make her whole life more rewarding."

One more example of how the hospital reaches into the community is the Witness to Violence program. Many of the kids Barry and the other professionals meet have been traumatized by seeing beatings, stabbings, and shootings—sometimes on the streets, sometimes within their own homes. The impact of this experience on a three-, four-, or five-year-old is profound and long-lasting, often revealing itself fully only years later, when the witness of abuse or violence may become a perpetrator of it.

The Witness to Violence program brings together community police officers with doctors, psychologists, and social workers from the hospital to discuss specific techniques for helping children cope with this kind of trauma. "We knew we needed to reach the police," Barry says, "because they're often the first ones on the scene when violence occurs. But we were afraid, when we started the program, that police officers wouldn't see the value in this training—that they'd think of it as some kind of soft-and-fuzzy social work rather than real policing. We were wrong," he explains. "It turned out that the police themselves were deeply concerned about the kids they met on the streets and eager to learn how to counsel and help them. They really appreciated getting the tools to make a difference at a terrible moment in a child's life."

Not every program that Barry and his colleagues develop is successful. He jokes, "Sometime I'll tell you about the fifteen other ideas that *didn't* work." But the innovation and experimentation never stops. The Boston Medical Center has become a vital center for community life because Barry Zuckerman and the other professionals there have chosen to expand their thinking beyond the traditional. Doctors and nurses don't just tend the body: They care for the minds, spirits, and souls of their patients, even when that means tackling such big issues as poverty, abuse, and violence. Not content to work around the margins, they're addressing problems head-on. Healthier kids, stronger families, and a more vital community are some of the results.

## Schools—Shapers of the Human Spirit

Because Dr. Zuckerman and his colleagues start with families and their needs, they've realized that community institutions—in health care, legal services, policing, and education—must find new ways to work together on behalf of families. Too often, families must negotiate a maze of conflicting, mutually uncomprehending bureaucracies in order to get the services they need. Those of us in positions of responsibility need to change that by making our neighborhood institutions into service centers that seamlessly connect people to the help they need.

No set of institutions can play a more pivotal role in this effort than our neighborhood schools. In many towns, they're the main centers of community life—sometimes the only place where everyone gets together to help, encourage, and nurture one another. Schools offer society a golden opportunity to provide kids and families with the resources they need in many areas of life— educationally, of course, but also in other aspects of their social, psychological, emotional, and physical health.

For many of us, a deep-rooted respect for schools and for education is a lifelong value. I'm certainly an example. As I was growing up, my parents always told me how important an education was for success in life. And I was lucky enough to have people around me who really pushed me to work hard and take advantage of every opportunity.

I was no genius, and my public-school education was good but not on a par with the rigorous precollege programs at private schools enjoyed by some of my fellow students at Northwestern University and the University of Michigan Law School. Consequently, I had to scramble during the early years at both schools to make good grades. At Michigan, I did nothing but study—in between the three part-time jobs I worked at to help pay the tuition bills.

Still, even to have access to higher education was a great stride for many in my generation. Neither of my parents finished high school; during their youth times were tough, and they had to go to work to help support their families. Maybe they valued education all the more as a result. One of the reasons I was able to succeed was that while I was in grade school my parents were there almost every evening of the week. They were members and supporters of the Parent-Teacher Association, the Mothers' and Fathers' Clubs, the Cub Scouts, and the Boy Scouts. It gave my brother Don and me a great deal of confidence to have our folks at school so frequently; the interest they took made us feel that what and how we learned was very important.

The same sense of nurturing and encouragement was reflected in our home life, too. When I was a child, my dad would come home from his milk route every afternoon around three o'clock. (The early quitting time was the only perk of his job; of course, his day *started* way before dawn!) Dad would settle into his favorite armchair, pull me on his lap, and read the daily newspaper to me, cover to cover. My favorite section was the comics, which he always read first; but he also covered the sports pages, the local news, business, politics—everything. I learned a great deal from those father-son reading sessions, but the most important lesson was that Dad cared for and respected me deeply enough to spend his afternoons reading aloud for my benefit.

I was also lucky enough to have a number of teachers who urged me on. Helen Baldwin, a teacher in my elementary school and a good friend of our family, was one of those. She was active in sports and played on my mother's volleyball team. She took a real interest in my brother and me and helped us with our studies. She coached me when I competed in the spelling bee and in another academic contest where I fielded questions with a team from my grade school against other schools. Miss Baldwin always talked about the importance of going to college and made a big impression on me and my parents in this regard.

Another person who influenced me greatly was Miss Thole, principal of my elementary school. She called my parents to a meeting at school around the time I was in the fifth grade, advising them that I was college material and that they should start saving money. She told them that going away to another city for college was a very important part of the learning experience. To this day, I doubt that I would have gone to college but for Miss Baldwin's and Miss Thole's advice to my parents.

My speech teacher, Miss Meenach, taught me public speaking, drama, and radio and television. (In those days, our school couldn't afford real broadcasting equipment, so we read scripts and improvised monologues while sitting in front of a make-believe microphone made of wood.) One day Miss Meenach asked me to stay after school. She told me about the High School Institute at Northwestern University, which would require five weeks during the summer between my junior and senior years. She offered to help me apply for a scholarship. I did apply, was accepted, and attended the Institute during the summer of 1957.

What an experience! I focused on drama that summer and played Henry Higgins in George Bernard Shaw's classic comedy *Pygmalion*. I met young people from all over the country who were the best students in drama, debate, and radio and television. Needless to say, after that wonderful summer I really wanted to attend Northwestern—and I did.

It wasn't easy for the Gephardts to send their children to college. Dad saved every penny he could, and my mother took a job as a secretary to help out. We also got a loan from a "revolving scholarship fund" at our church: $500 per semester on condition that we repay the money when we could. Since there were virtually no college loans or grants available at that time, it was the church's help, along with our three part-time jobs, that really made it possible for us to attend college. Supporting education was a mission that every institution in the community took seriously.

I will never forget how many people—my parents, teachers, principals, church members—helped me get a good education. My passion for education and children, and improving both, comes from these experiences.

## Family Realities in the Year 2000

It's pleasant to wax nostalgic about the supportive and nurturing families and communities that carried us to adulthood. Unfortunately, nostalgia is no basis for thinking about the current and future challenges our families face. Too often, we think about child-raising and education as if the year were 1950 rather than 2000.

In truth, family life—which is at the heart of both child rearing and education—has fundamentally changed for most American families. Today about half of all marriages end in divorce, which often leaves single parents attempting to carry out the responsibilities of a couple. Many parents—married or single—work two jobs or carry a lot of overtime to make ends meet. The resulting shortfall in time for family and community life is a quiet crisis we have yet to fully acknowledge.

I recently met a young man as I went door to door, visiting homes in my Missouri district—I'll call him Greg. He was obviously in a hurry, but he was willing to chat for a minute. "What do you do?" I asked.

"Which job?" Greg asked.

"Both of them, I guess," I replied. Greg explained that he worked from seven in the morning till noon as a clerk at an auto-parts shop; then he worked as a janitor at his kids' school from two in the afternoon till eleven at night.

I was a bit appalled. "When do you see your family?" I asked.

"Actually, never. On the weekends, I'm at my *third* job."

Not everyone is stretched quite that thin, but a lot of us are. Even people with prestigious, relatively high paying jobs are working longer hours than ever, for the reasons I discussed earlier in this book: global competition, the electronic information revolution, and the heightened pace of change. According to one study, parents today spend 40 percent *less time* with their children than they did just a generation ago. Yet as policymakers and even as parents we seem not to notice this fundamental change, and we tend to act and think as if it had never happened.

Children don't raise themselves. If families aren't adequately raising all of our children due to time and financial pressures, then society must find ways, in its own self-interest, to help. The signs of our failure to do so thus far are obvious and ominous. In my home state of Missouri, the thorniest budget issue of late has been how to finance more prison cells to house the anticipated increase in the Missouri prison population, estimated to balloon from roughly 15,000 inmates to 30,000 inmates during the next few years. Each cell costs nearly $40,000 to construct, and it costs $27,000 per year to hold someone in prison. Of course, we have to be tough on crime, but we can't afford our current Band-Aid approach to the social problems caused by inadequate parenting.

How and when do kids start getting into trouble with the law? According to the Department of Justice, more than 50 percent of all juvenile crime occurs between two o'clock in the afternoon and eight o'clock in the evening. It's understandable: Those are the hours between when children are let out of school and when their parents get home from work. Many are unsupervised—not because they have bad parents but because there often is no other choice. The cost of day care or an after-school program—if it's available at all—is out of reach for far too many.

We're thus caught in a deadly spiral: The more we neglect the educational and social needs of families, the higher the ultimate costs we end up paying. During a visit to San Francisco, I met with Waldemar Rojas, the superintendent of the school system. He told me that in recent years, more than 10,000 of California's college and university professors have been laid off to save money. During the same time, the state hired more than 10,000 prison guards. And with overtime and fringe benefits, the guards make more than the professors did!

Congressman Charlie Rangel of New York, a good friend of mine, has pointed out for years the shortsighted approach we take to education. We'd be a lot better off, Charlie insists, if we spent our money training kids for the job market rather than absorbing the costs that undereducated youth inflict on society in the long term. As Jesse Jackson rightly says, "It's Yale or jail."

In the United States today, we have more than 1.7 million people behind bars, far more than in any other industrialized nation. The costs are astronomical. This is a symptom of the strains and stresses our families and communities fall under due to the radical economic and social changes of the past fifty years. We need to take a long, realistic look at those changes before we can begin to diagnose the problems and formulate solutions.

# The Global Challenge

In addition to our huge prison population, we have millions of other citizens who are unemployed because they lack training or education. There is still a strong, direct link between education level and compensation, and American businesses are woefully short of highly trained workers. In Silicon Valley today, there are thousands of jobs that cannot be filled adequately by Americans, including more than 1,500 at Microsoft alone; there are approximately 300,000 such jobs nationally. Employers have been urging Congress to loosen U.S. immigration policies to bring in more workers from India and China to fill these jobs. There's nothing wrong with welcoming immigrants to our shores, but we should be able to fill these jobs with students from our own schools—or, if our system isn't producing qualified candidates, we've got to fix it.

I often tell students in my congressional district that they will be competing in business, whether they know it or not, against workers in China, India, and Brazil. High-technology is now available anywhere on the globe; there are very few manufacturing and service activities that cannot be done almost anywhere on earth.

Several years ago, I traveled to the Far East to study firsthand the challenges we face. I visited a factory in Thailand that produces the hard disks that go into computers sold here and around the world. These are some of today's most advanced technology products, produced to exacting tolerances. When we entered the factory, we were asked to put on lint- and dust-free garments, including covers for our shoes. The workrooms were pressurized so that when the doors were opened, the air would rush out, pushing dust and dirt out as well. This was the same clean-room technology and procedure that I had seen in California's Silicon Valley and in high-tech factories across the United States.

But the workers at the factory in Thailand were making just a few dollars per day. That's the competition our firms and our workers are up against.

I asked the plant manager about his employees. He was very proud of them. They worked hard without complaining, he said; and the turnover in his plant was extremely low in comparison to other facilities in the area because this plant offered free transportation to work and other benefits.

As employees, he said, they had only one weakness—but that was a significant one: "Throw them a curve ball, and they're lost." You could teach them any task, and they would perform it as reliably as anyone. But if you asked them to adapt—to use their minds creatively and with initiative to solve unexpected problems—they couldn't do it.

It isn't that Thai workers aren't good, smart people—they are. They work hard to provide for themselves and their families, seeking many of the same things from life that we do. The primary differences are that they lack the education that our best workers benefit from and that their culture stresses discipline rather than creativity.

So we have little advantage in technology over our competitors in Thailand, yet we cannot hope to compete with them as low-cost producers. Our only edge—if we can maintain it—lies in the energetic, information-fueled creativity of our workforce.

The same is true all around the world. In Mexico, just miles from the U.S. border, you'll see high-tech plants where productivity matches that of many U.S. facilities. But the workers make less than a dollar an hour and live in horrid living conditions. If we are to meet that competition, we must have even better educated workers who can perform more sophisticated tasks with less supervision and greater levels of innovation—for which they can be paid far more than a dollar an hour.

This, then, is the nature of the global challenge we face. If we are going to maintain and increase our standard of living, we've got to be that much more creative, productive, and entrepreneurial than our international competitors. As boundaries of time and distance are leveled by technological advances, the one thing that distinguishes us is our people.

Not all of public education is failing, but there are real signs of increasing failure that must be taken seriously. More than one in ten of our students drop out before graduating high school. And today, even graduates often have deficient skills in math and English.

Several years ago, I visited the Motorola Corporation's facilities in Schaumburg, Illinois. I learned from Motorola's human-resources officials that they were having trouble finding people with the basic skills needed to qualify for entry-level jobs. Of the people who took the application tests, roughly two out of three failed. The remaining 33 percent who had the basic qualifications just to get through the door often needed additional company training before they could be put to work.

Though crucial, better education alone will not guarantee success. Today's workers must have social skills as well as intellectual ones, because much of today's most advanced and productive work requires skilled teams working together creatively. In the long run, there's no doubt that our people are up to both tasks. But if we are to make progress on this most important challenge, we have to change our thinking about both child-raising and education.

## "Victory Is in the Classroom"

Some time ago, I visited the Seattle school system. I'd heard good things about the new superintendent, General John Stanford (a great man who, I'm sorry to say, recently passed away). John had been General Colin Powell's deputy during the 1991 Gulf War, responsible for logistical support for our troops. He had no experience in administering a school system. But he did have one vital characteristic: He was a leader. He knew how to understand a challenge, how to marshal the resources to respond, and how to provide the leadership necessary to make changes happen.

Like so many public-school systems today, the Seattle system is a multicultural challenge. More than fifty different languages are spoken, and a surprising percentage of the students are homeless. I visited an elementary school with John and was astonished to see that many kids arrived and left in taxis each day, picked up from the shelters and the vans and cars that their families lived in.

John talked about how important education was and why he had chosen to take on this challenge. The military, he believed, is a perfect training ground for an educator in terms of leadership and focus. If our military's job is to defend the country against the threats we face, surely the biggest threat we now face is the problem of producing young adults who can succeed and prosper in today's world.

John said something that has stuck with me ever since: "The victory is in the classroom." During the 1950s and 1960s we measured the strength of our nation in nuclear megatons, but in the next century we will measure it by the number of our people who are literate, educated, and trained.

John's motto: "There aren't any throwaway kids anymore." It's true in Seattle, and throughout America. But we need to act on it, in every town and in every classroom.

# Nostalgia and Silver Bullets

To deal effectively with this problem of raising and educating children for the next century, we must reach a consensus about the difficulties we face. Nostalgia hinders this effort. When the facts about how much less time parents spend with children are cited, many people conclude that our challenge is to figure out how to get more parents to stay at home raising children. Some argue that women should resume their historical role as full-time homemakers, whereas others argue for changes in the economy that would encourage more stay-at-home parenting. Both ideas are rooted in the premise that the 1950s-style *Leave It to Beaver* household can somehow be resurrected.

Unfortunately, nostalgia no more meets our current challenge than wishing that Pearl Harbor had never been attacked would have helped us in 1941. The economic and social forces that have revolutionized our family lives can not be reversed. If we avoid changing our way of thinking and our institutions to deal with the problems so created, we'll simply make the real solutions harder to achieve.

Today, most families simply don't have the choices that many middle-class Americans once had. Most families now need two breadwinners to live the good life. And each of the jobs we take on is likely to be more responsible, more challenging, more of a round-the-clock effort than the jobs our parents held decades ago. For all of us, time is at a premium.

Let me add that many of the changes in our economy have been good ones. The standard of middle-class living is far higher today than it was during the 1950s and 1960s. Millions take for granted the second car, the third TV set, the spacious family room, and the summer vacation that would have been luxuries to their parents—not to mention the many products that didn't even exist a generation ago, from VCRs and CD players to home computers and microwave ovens. And the steady flow of women, including mothers, into our workplaces has brought them a degree of independence and freedom that's in the best American tradition of expanding opportunity and democracy. Even if we could, we wouldn't want to return to the old days when Mom had no choice but to stay home, keeping house for Dad and the kids.

Still, many families today would like greater freedom of choice where work is concerned. Especially when children are small, many mothers and fathers would like to shorten their work hours without drastically reducing the family's standard of living. For most people, it's not a realistic option, and we gain nothing by pretending it is. Until our economy grows at a faster pace and prosperity is more broadly shared—so that everyone has a chance to reach the winner's circle—we have to accept the fact that American families today are badly stretched and find ways to deal with that reality.

Another common reaction to the problems of child-rearing and education is to tinker around the edges with small efforts and partial answers that look and sound appealing but do not address the broad challenges we face. Mandatory school uniforms, metal detectors, reduced class sizes, teacher testing, the downsizing of central school bureaucracies, the wiring of schools for the Internet—all are examples of ideas that may have merit and may need to be part of a larger effort, but will not achieve the kind of substantial progress we need.

Another distraction is the suggestion that we can solve our schools' problems by giving vouchers to public-school students to help them pay the cost of private and parochial schools. Private education is often excellent, but it's hard to understand how draining needed moneys from public schools is going to solve the problems those schools have. I don't object to considering how public moneys can be used to deliver certain limited services to private and parochial school students. But the facts are clear: The vast majority of American students have always been educated in public schools and probably always will be. The solutions must be found in the public schools, not elsewhere.

## Schools That Work

If we could reach a national consensus on the causes of human dysfunction, we might be able to launch fruitful efforts to solve the problem. A good place to start is to examine schools and school systems that are getting good results in today's reality.

One such school is Central Park East School in New York City. The school is in the heart of Harlem—one of the toughest neighborhoods in New York City and, indeed, the country.

Walking through the door for my first visit, I was quickly struck by the fact that there were no metal detectors or police guards, unlike at other inner-city schools. Paul Schwarz, the principal at the time, told me that he would quit before he would install a metal detector. He said, "We *know* all of our kids, and we know their parents—and I can guarantee you that none of them would ever think of bringing a weapon to this school." To me, the absence of metal detectors was a remarkable sign of the trust that exists at the school—that the students of Central Park East will do nothing to spoil the rich learning environment they and their teachers have created.

The school was started in 1984 by Deborah Meier, an ordinary teacher who became a true educational visionary and an apostle of *true caring* as a key to school success. Paul Schwarz was Deborah's codirector and continued to follow her model. Shortly after I sat down for a visit in Paul's office, a student knocked on his door, saying that she had a problem. In most schools I've been in, the principal would have brushed her aside, and might even have become angry for being interrupted during a visit with an important politician. Not Paul. He excused himself and talked to the student. It was clear where his priority was—and that showed me everything.

At Central Park East, students achieve high standards through a variety of common-sense efforts. The original concept was to restrict the overall size of the school to two hundred students. However, the school building is large enough for many more students than that, so the institution is physically and administratively divided into several smaller divisions, each a "school" with a maximum of two hundred students. Paul said, "Students who come from difficult family situations give up and drop out in huge high school factories, where they are anonymous and lose their already-diminished sense of identity."

Each student develops a special relationship with one teacher for two or three years—sometimes the first sustained relationship with an adult in the student's life. This is made possible by the small size of the school divisions, and it works for the students on several levels, not least of which is the high academic achievement it fosters. Paul Schwarz explains:

> Schools are not created to be "comfortable" places for children and teachers; they are meant to be places of rigorous instruction and lots of learning. If you care about teaching students to be thoughtful, you have to know what they are thinking, and you cannot do that unless you can find ways to *listen* to them. That's why we created a schedule that ensures that no teacher ever teaches more than forty students, as opposed to the 150 students most American teachers have at any one time.

The sense of intimacy also adds to the safety of the school. After tragic school shootings occurred in several American towns during 1998, educators conducted focus groups to figure out how schools could be made safer. Paul notes that when students were asked about this issue they said, "Know our names!" When every student is known and cared about by at least one adult, troubled kids are much less likely to fall through the cracks.

Finally, the faculty ditched the central curriculum concocted by the notorious New York Board of Education bureaucracy and created its own program. The Central Park East curriculum demands exceedingly advanced thinking standards as part of learning any subject matter, along with serious, high-standard written and oral exams during senior year.

Not unlike the progressive businesses we visited in Part 1 of this book, Central Park East is proud of the fact that it actively uses the creativity and intelligence of all its employees—not just desig-nated "leaders." As Paul Schwarz notes, "We are a staff-run school because we believe that when teachers know they are 'owners,' they are willing to work differently for the school. So Central Park East is a 'Mom-and-Pop *bodega*' rather than a McDonald's franchise."

Student Damary Bonilla joined us during my visit that day—a dynamic young girl who, I suspect, is destined to be a real success in life. She shared with me her "portfolios," products of her learn-ing that were presented to a group of teachers and others to deter-mine her grades. In some ways, the presentation of a portfolio is much like a graduate student's defense of her doctoral disserta-tion. The quality of the work was impressive, reflecting not only the school's rigorous standards but also the sense of pride that comes with surviving any tough, shared challenge—like Marine Basic Training.

The results achieved by Central Park East are fantastic. During the first thirteen years of operation, the total number of students who dropped out was eleven—a stunningly low number. And 90 percent or more of the students go on to college.

Another school that gets remarkable results is the Affton-Lind-bergh Early Childhood Education School in Missouri. Fifteen years ago, a mother named Cathy Strup-Davis took it upon herself to bring change to an inner-suburban school district. The im-provements that she and her allies have gradually brought about are impressive. The school has become a successful center for Par-ents as Teachers, a nationwide program that provides parent edu-cation, child development, and family support. The school also has a full pre-school (for which a modest tuition is charged), be-fore and after school programs from three to six o'clock every afternoon, and a summer camp program. As a result, Affton-Lindbergh is an extremely popular school, and families from around the area vie for homes that will permit their children to attend it.

I visited Affton-Lindbergh School one Saturday when it had a special program for parents with young children, an extension of the Parents as Teachers Program. Sheila Sherman, the program's founder, explained the concept to me. It's based on three principles: First, that children begin learning at birth and do their most important developing *before* they enter school; second, that parents are therefore their children's first teachers; and third, that parents want to be *good* parents and teachers.

"It makes so much sense to train young parents about their responsibility as parents," Sherman explained. "Instead, we just assume that they know what to do without being taught. In fact, we train people for everything *but* parenthood. We give high school students more training for driving cars than we give them for being parents!

"Parents as Teachers also provides a natural lead-in to the preschool program. It makes the school a real family center and the nexus for many social activities, really getting the parents involved in their child's education."

I was reminded of my parents' deep involvement with my schooling so many years ago at Mason School. Affton-Lindbergh has created similar results in a very different world through the use of a variety of optional programs that help parents be parents in the modern age. It's one thing to lecture parents on their responsibilities. It's quite another thing to really *help* them to understand and carry out those responsibilities.

Parents as Teachers has been a real success. In an independent evaluation, children participating in the program scored significantly higher on all measures of intelligence achievement, verbal ability, hearing comprehension, and language abilities. Participating children were more frequently described by their parents as having a strong sense of self, positive relationships with adults, and coping capabilities. And the number of children in the program who entered first grade needing remedial or special education was less than half that of nonparticipating youngsters in Missouri.

Furthermore, there's evidence that these successes endure. In a follow-up study, participating children were significantly ahead of their nonparticipating peers in academic performance at the end of first grade. And, just as important, the follow-up study reported that participating parents continued to play a more active role in their children's learning and formal schooling than did nonparticipating parents.

I was so impressed with Parents as Teachers that I joined my Republican Senate colleague from Missouri, Kit Bond, in introducing legislation in Congress to expand the program to other states. It hasn't yet passed, but the effort goes on.

Another school I like to point to is Shepard School in inner-city St. Louis. Their standardized test scores, grades, awards, and scholarships won all show marked signs of improvement and high achievement. I asked Carol Hall-Whittier, the principal, how she was getting such good results in the kind of neighborhood many educators despair of. She answered, "Well, we do all the obvious things that parents, especially single parents, need today. We have Parents as Teachers, preschool, after-school, and summer-school programs. But the most important thing we do is to really get the parents involved in their children's education."

I asked how they did that. "Well," she said, "at the start of the school year, I sent a letter to each parent saying I expected them to spend one hour a week in the school with their children and the teachers. Most of the parents came, but a few didn't. So I went out to their houses and told them that the letter was *mandatory*, not optional."

Impressed and a little shocked at her nerve, I asked her where she got the power to do this. She said, "Nobody *told* me I could do it—I just *did* it!"

A young mother listening to the story piped up: "*I* am one of the parents she visited. I'm a single mom, and I work the night shift—from midnight till eight in the morning. I was *not* excited about getting up early to come to school, believe me! And the truth is," she continued, "I was also embarrassed to come. You see, I never graduated from grade school myself. But after the principal visited, I thought I *had* to come—after all, she said so. So the next day I went, and I've been coming every day ever since—all day."

Summing up her feelings on parent involvement, she said, "My coming to school has made a big difference in my two kids. They see me here, and they know that what they're doing is really important. They're getting much better grades than they used to. But you know what else?"—and she laughed—"I now feel that *all* of these children are *my* children!"

If everyone connected with our kids and schools could get the exact same feeling, the problem of raising children properly would be on the way to being solved. The schools I've talked about, and many others, have some of the answers. But the same approaches won't work everywhere. The question is not only how to promote change at the local level and how to develop leaders who can guide teachers, administrators, parents, students, and communities through these changes; the question is also how we can bring about a nationwide renaissance in our schools—how we can take positive change and "bring it to scale."

## Pushing the System to Respond

A problem of this magnitude requires everyone to take personal responsibility for solving it. It is a family issue, a community issue, a national issue. Our most important national goal must be to ensure that every American child becomes a productive, contributing member of our society—almost the way our overriding goal during World War II was simply to win the war. Just as Pearl Harbor made clear a potentially fatal threat to our nation's future, today more than a million and a half people in prison and millions of untrained and unproductive workers present a different but equally dangerous threat.

We've seen other "wars" since World War II. The War on Poverty during the 1960s, the War on Drugs during the 1980s, and the War on Crime during the 1990s all achieved some successes, but none achieved overwhelming victory as our armed forces did in 1945. Probably our most impressive national effort since World War II was when President John F. Kennedy challenged the country to land a man on the moon within a decade. A huge effort was put in place to enhance math and science education from elementary schools on up. And it worked: Neil Armstrong walked on the lunar surface in 1969, right on schedule. The American people responded magnificently to a challenge and to dynamic national leadership.

Right now, we have a living example of a community responding to leadership to improve education in one of our biggest cities.

A few years ago, Mayor Richard M. Daley of Chicago realized the importance of public schools to maintaining a vibrant urban community. More and more young families were leaving Chicago because they did not like its public schools, taking their tax base with them to the suburbs. As a result, Daley saw schools, neighborhoods, and an entire city in decline.

Concerned, even angry, Daley took action. He went to the Illinois state legislature and asked for the responsibility—the "ownership," if you will—of running the Chicago public schools. He put his most talented and trusted aides in charge. They closed underperforming schools and reopened them with new teachers and administrators. They ended "social promotions," demanding real achievement to get to the next grade or to graduate.

The experiment is still in its early stages, but there is already an air of expectation in Chicago about public schools; the exodus of families from the city may finally be ending. This passion to do a better job of raising and educating children that Mayor Daley exhibits must be shared ultimately by every citizen if we are to meet our nation's number-one challenge. To really win tomorrow's "victory in the classroom," we must take responsibility—personal, institutional, community, and national responsibility—for fighting and winning the war:

- First, we must take responsibility as parents to spend time and effort raising and nurturing our children in body, mind, and spirit.

- Second, whether or not we are parents, we must take responsibility to make sure our local public schools are doing all they can to educate our children.

- Third, as citizens of communities and the nation, we must take responsibility to ensure that we have enough skilled, well-trained, caring teachers for all our children.

- Fourth, we must take responsibility to see that our federal government provides the educational resources needed to supplement what state and local governments can offer.

- Fifth, we must take responsibility for reforming how we teach, replacing the factory model with schools that offer kids the personal attention and nurturing they need.

- Sixth, we must take responsibility for bringing higher education within the financial reach of every American family.

## Success Starts at Home

Let's talk first about what parents can do to better raise and educate our children.

First, a seemingly simple thing that's so very important: Read to your children. I think reading to our kids was the best thing Jane and I ever did for them. Some books they insisted on hearing over and over again, especially their favorite Dr. Seuss classics, *The Cat in the Hat* and *The Grinch Who Stole Christmas*. Truth be told, Jane and I enjoyed the stories almost as much as our kids; we'd laugh and laugh about the antics of those crazy characters. And I think the kids felt the same closeness to Jane and me that I felt when my own father pulled me up on his lap every day to read me the newspaper cover to cover.

Second, help your kids with their homework and take an interest in what they're doing in school. Don't do the work for them, but just asking how it's going and offering occasional help when they're stumped is very welcome. I spent many a night with one of our kids at the local library, helping with research on a tough paper. Sure, this hard-working student could have finished the work alone, but it was a very big deal to have Dad there, lending confidence and support.

Third, try to make it to every open-school night, parent-teacher conference, or school committee meeting, and, if you can, spend an hour a week in your kids' school as a volunteer. The story of Shepard School in St. Louis shows the importance of parent involvement. Every school has dozens of ways, big and small, that you can help: tutoring students in reading or math, going along on class trips to the zoo or the local museum, helping with art projects, and many others. If necessary, ask your employer for flexibility in your work schedule so you can take time to be with your child in school. When you get that flexibility, give your employers the public praise they deserve so the policy will continue for you and other parents.

Fourth, just spend time with your children. You can give them no greater gift. When our kids were young, Jane and I especially enjoyed taking part of a day to spend alone with a single child—skating, or at the movies, or at a ballgame. The activity didn't matter as much as taking time to do something alone with that child. It gave us time to talk about what they were doing, what they were worried about, what they feared, what made them happy. Above all, it showed respect, love, and concern for them as a fellow human being—something we all need and want.

If every parent did these four simple things, it would lead to substantial progress in addressing our education and child-raising problems. And a large percentage of our crime, drug, and alcohol-abuse problems would begin to abate as well. It's not a matter of being there for your kids once or twice a year or when there's nothing better to do. It has to be a lifetime approach, given the same priority as work and the other things that matter most to you.

The American Federation of Teachers (AFT) has helped lead many significant efforts for school reform. Although some Republicans enjoy denouncing the AFT and other teachers' unions, the fact is that most teachers are hard-working, dedicated people doing one of the most difficult and important jobs in the country. But the AFT's own research has made it clear that education starts and ends at home.

One analysis revealed that "three factors controllable by parents—student absenteeism, variety of reading materials at home, excessive television watching—explained almost 90 percent of the difference in eighth-grade math test scores across 37 states and Washington, D.C." Other research has shown that by the age of three, children have acquired *more than half* of their lifetime language skills. Parents are, indeed, a child's first teachers.

In addition to being a good parent at home, you can take a leadership role to improve your local public schools if they are deficient. Remember the stories of how Cathy Strup-Davis, a neighborhood parent, helped turn around the Affton School, and how Debbie Meier, a rank-and-file teacher, led the reinvention of Central Park East in Harlem. When we're unhappy with our kids' schools, it's all too easy to gripe and backbite from the sidelines. Instead, apply the same energy to organizing, suggesting, and promoting improvements. So many others have made a real difference—you can, too.

## Befriending Your Community's Schools

The efforts of parents and teachers alone will not allow us to win the education war. Everybody can and must do something to help. Community involvement in supporting our schools is in the best tradition of American volunteerism—and, in truth, it can be deeply gratifying for those who give their time and talent.

One of the most important things you can do is to volunteer to be a mentor to public-school students. Many public schools have after-school programs for which mentors are needed, but if your local school does not have a mentoring program, try starting one. You'll be amazed what an hour or two a week can do for a youngster who may not have the advantage of an actively involved parent.

Craig Hanna, a member of my staff for more than a decade, is involved with a fantastic program in Washington, D.C. called Horton's Kids (named after Dr. Seuss's lovable elephant who faithfully nurtured a neglected egg). Volunteers take kids to ballgames and museums as well as for checkups at the doctor and the dentist. I've seen with my own eyes how the kids respond to the friendship and respect they're given by the volunteers. And I've seen how fulfilling the program is for Craig—despite working twelve- to fourteen-hour days, he always makes time for the kids. Several other members of my staff in Washington and St. Louis devote considerable time to volunteer work as well.

If you have a little more time, consider volunteering for the local school board or for committees working to pass bond issues or tax propositions for the local schools. This is vitally important, challenging work, especially in today's unthinking, antitax atmosphere. In my own congressional district, the Affton School District, despite its broad support among parents and families, recently lost two bond issues that would have raised badly needed money to repair the schools—by margins of only thirty-two votes and eleven votes!

Passing school bond issues in Missouri takes a supermajority, making it very difficult to raise the money our schools need, but everywhere social factors conspire against the schools, too. Many parents of school-age kids feel too busy to vote, whereas senior citizens, with more time on their hands, often vote no because their own kids are out of school. A few nonparent volunteers working on behalf of school funding out of pure public-spiritedness can make the difference between success and failure.

You may want to volunteer to recruit other people, especially senior citizens, to help out at school with mentoring, tutoring, and special projects. In my congressional district, I meet hundreds of senior citizens who say they are bored. Some sit at home, nervously watching the local news, which often exaggerates the amount of juvenile crime in the community. If they would give a couple of hours a week to the schools, not only would they enjoy a proactive role in preventing the juvenile crime they fear but they might even find they actually *like* the youngsters they get to know.

Consider organizing a fund-raising drive for the public school you graduated from. It's a funny thing: I get fund-raising appeals from Northwestern University and the University of Michigan Law School almost every month. Why shouldn't Mason School or Southwest High School, which surely contributed at least as much to my later life, have an endowment fund just as the universities do? John Stanford developed this very idea in Seattle. He got some of his public schools to contact their outstanding alums to launch private fund-raising drives. They amazed themselves with their success. Some public schools have thousands of alums, many of whom are quite successful and would gladly give money to help their old schools. Why not volunteer to get the ball rolling on behalf of your own alma mater?

# Where Are Tomorrow's Teachers?

The vast majority of teachers are dedicated, caring, and competent people who entered the profession out of a desire to make a difference in a child's life. They certainly didn't do it for the money.

But today we're facing a crisis in teaching. Right now, there are about 2.6 million teachers in the United States. Over the next decade, however, so many are expected to retire or leave the profession that we will need to hire more than 2.2 million new teachers. And we're just about to experience the effects of the baby boom echo, as children of the huge postwar generation flood our schools. Serious teacher shortages are the likely result.

As part of his 1998 legislative program, President Clinton wisely focused on getting 100,000 more teachers into communities across the country. Just as putting 100,000 more police officers on the streets has already helped to reduce the crime rate, 100,000 more teachers in the schools will allow us to reduce class sizes so that kids can get more individualized attention. But adding 100,000 more teaching positions when we're already losing millions of teachers raises the stakes even more. The teacher shortage is already reaching crisis proportions. States are bidding against each other to attract new teachers. Massachusetts, for example, has offered a $20,000 bonus to draw new teacher candidates, and other states are having to follow suit. It's great for the teachers—but bad for school systems that can't afford to keep pace.

In addition, schools now hire teachers who are not qualified to teach because of the shortage. I'm told that in Los Angeles public schools, for example, roughly half of the teachers do not have their teaching certificate because they have a college degree, but no significant training in teaching skills.

Difficult working conditions compound the problem. Twenty-two percent of all teachers leave the profession within the first three years; for teachers in urban schools, the rate reaches almost 50 percent. To attract and keep good teachers, we have to pay them a decent salary and strive to improve the conditions they teach in. A teacher with thirty students can't reach the kids individually no matter how much he or she is paid; neither can a teacher whose classroom is in disrepair or one who lacks textbooks and basic supplies.

Teachers need help from their colleagues, too. We should expand peer review of teachers to help identify classroom problems before they become too great, to provide training where it's needed, and to ensure that people who simply weren't meant to teach find some other calling in life.

Teacher testing may also have a role to play. If suitable tests can be developed to help judge members of the teaching profession, we should look carefully at implementing them. As we improve pay and working conditions for teachers, their accountability should also be increased.

Let's also expand our concept of who we consider to be teachers. As I travel the country, some of the best educational programs I see involve schools partnering with the private sector. Mentoring, internship, and similar programs can help problem and at-risk children profoundly by providing a meaningful context for what they're learning in school. When they see how a subject relates to real-world activities in business, health care, the arts, and elsewhere, they return to the classroom with a new sense of purpose.

I saw a great example of this at Cambridge Rindge and Latin, a vocational school where my friend Larry Rosenstock was the principal. Although many people think of Cambridge, Massachusetts, as the place where the professors from Harvard and MIT live, it's mainly a blue-collar community with many of the same problems found in such communities all across the country.

When I visited Cambridge Rindge and Latin, Larry's students eagerly told me about their internships in companies around the city. Some worked at nearby Polaroid, others in real-estate offices, still others in Boston city government agencies. They were proud of what they were learning and had gained priceless insights into what it would take for them to succeed in their later work lives.

I visited the school woodworking shop, where students had made sets of interlocking gears out of wood. By studying gear ratios to determine how power was generated and transmitted through these simple machines, the students were coming to see the realities behind the arcane math formulas they'd been studying. They were excited about what they were learning because they saw how it all fit together.

One student I met happily described her work for a real-estate firm, where she'd been helping with basic office work and computerized record-keeping. She talked proudly about how the people of the firm had taken an interest in her and how they'd come to trust her—so much so, she said, that they'd given her a key to the office so she could open up early. She took out the key to show us, gravely displaying it as a symbol of the respect and dignity she'd earned. Now she wanted to excel at school—for herself, for her family, and for her coworkers; all were deeply interested in her success.

In cities and towns around the country, progressive employers are encouraging employees to spend time in local schools, often giving paid time off to make it possible. Programs vary from just a couple of hours a year to full days of volunteer work, sometimes with company donations of money, products, services, and equipment as additional help.

Some companies have even "adopted" neighborhood schools, developing long-term commitments that strengthen local education, improve the flow of talented graduates into the business community, and enrich the lives of all those who participate. Businesspeople like Gary Hirschberg, the head of Stonyfield Yogurt in New Hampshire, have told me how rewarding it is to become a partner in education through school adoption. Why not suggest it at the company where you work?

# Washington's Role

The federal government has always had a supporting role in public education, helping in areas where local school districts need it. For instance, back in the 1950s, while many local schools had trouble affording a school-lunch program the federal government was stockpiling excess agricultural products. It made sense to match the need with the supply, so the federal government stepped in to play a big role in lunch and, eventually, breakfast programs. To this day, the federal government pays most or all of the cost of providing a free breakfast and lunch to poor children in schools. It's a sensible policy—and a very affordable one.

The federal government helps education in other ways. During the 1960s, Uncle Sam started paying school districts additional funds for poor and disadvantaged youngsters through the so-called Title I program. And millions have been helped with financing higher education through federal programs for college loans and grants.

These programs are a start, but the federal government needs to do more to help local schools. As I mentioned, we've agreed to fund 100,000 new teachers for our public schools to provide for smaller class sizes in grades one through three. And the Clinton administration is trying to use federal dollars to help local school districts pay the interest costs on school construction bonds. If that help could be offered, local school districts could more easily borrow money to build the extra classrooms they need to actually achieve smaller class sizes. We must also fully fund Head Start and make it available for younger children. I believe these efforts—more teachers, more classrooms, and reaching out to prepare students to learn—are an appropriate way for the federal government to help local public schools cope with the massive changes they face each day.

Rebuilding our educational infrastructure is another urgent need that is just too big and too pervasive for purely local solutions. The truth is that there is a larger number of children entering the school systems in our country in the year 2000 than anytime in our history. Yet many of our school buildings were constructed many years ago and are inadequate to accommodate the number of students entering our schools. Traveling around the country, I'm often startled at the state of disrepair in so many of our schools. In Washington, D.C., many schools couldn't open for the 1998 school year because of a court order requiring basic repairs to protect the safety of the students. (Imagine—a judge must intervene so that kids can sit in a classroom without fearing that the roof will fall in on them.) In the South, I've seen school after school in need of major repairs, most lacking air-conditioning. How can kids focus on their studies in the stifling heat of June in Georgia and Texas? And what message do we send to our children about the importance of education if their schools are crumbling around them as they try to learn?

The General Accounting Office figures we need more than $100 billion to rebuild our nation's schools to ensure a safe, secure learning environment. Yet Congress has refused to commit the necessary money. Republicans repeatedly fought our efforts to make even a small down payment of $5 billion to address the very worst problems. This year's budget finally includes some money, but much, much more is needed.

The resources needed to upgrade our schools for the twenty-first century are another story. Across the country, local communities are scrambling to wire their schools to the Internet. Many local businesses are donating time, money, and equipment to provide the access to technology that our kids need. It was a sad joke when former House Speaker Newt Gingrich proposed giving every homeless kid a laptop computer: How about first providing a room with a roof overhead and a place to plug in a computer? But Newt was right about the importance of connecting our kids to the newest technology, and he was right to suggest that a national effort is required.

Finally, we need new and creative ways to use federal aid to reward and help schools that are getting good results despite all the new problems.

Education shouldn't be a partisan issue—but increasingly it is. On one side are Republicans, who believe that the public schools are so poorly run, that the teachers and their unions are so incompetent, that they want to give up on public education. They want to privatize schools, giving every family a voucher they can use to shop around for the school of their choice. A "free market in education" is their answer to every problem in our schools.

The problem with the Republican idea is that in every free market huge class discrepancies are inevitable. When there are no more public schools, those with plenty of money will be able to buy a better education for their kids; the rest will get by with whatever third-rate product they can afford. I don't think that's the kind of system Americans really want.

There's another reason—a civic reason—for supporting public schools. Public education is one of the greatest tools ever invented for building a unified civil society. In public schools, kids from different backgrounds—kids of every race, religion, ethnicity, income, and family circumstance—come together to learn from their teachers and from each other. I treasured the experience of going to public schools and making friends from every walk of life, and so have my children.

As common ground for all our people, America's public schools historically have taught civility, tolerance, and mutual understanding along with math, history, and science. They've been a primary ingredient in our long-term success as a nation, and we should be very leery of proposals—like today's voucher schemes—that could weaken our commitment to them.

A better approach is to reform the public schools, rewarding and expanding the programs that work and junking the ones that don't. Scapegoating schools and educators isn't fair or helpful. Most are doing the best they can, often against tremendous odds.

At the same time, we can do a lot better. I and my liberal Democratic friends have often been accused of throwing money at problems—and sometimes we've been guilty as charged. Let's acknowledge that money alone won't solve our educational problems and that it is time to abandon approaches that don't demand results.

## Rewards for Results

I hear a lot of complaints from homeowners around the country about being asked to pay higher property taxes to support local schools. Although a few folks will always object to paying taxes, most people understand that taxes are necessary; they simply want to know that their money is being put to good use. Most people aren't selfish, but they are self-interested. They don't want their money wasted, and they're right to feel that way.

For several years I've advocated an approach I call Rewards for Results. It's based on the common-sense idea that if you want better results you should provide incentives for achieving them. Under this approach, schools and school districts that improve in measurable ways would be rewarded with additional funds to build on their successes.

It's an approach that differs from both the old liberal orthodoxy ("Let's create another federal agency") and the current conservative dogma ("Let the free market take care of it"). It's a practical approach focused on specific goals, one that puts our dollars to work in programs where they'll be well and wisely spent.

The practical core of this program is a set of bonus payments available to state and local governments that achieve certain basic objectives. For example, a bonus would be payable to a state for each child who arrives on the schoolhouse steps for first grade properly nourished, with all of her shots, and with a background of early childhood education that makes her ready to learn beginning on day one. How each state will achieve these goals will be up to each state individually; local educators don't need the federal government micromanaging their school districts. But Uncle Sam should work with states, localities, and educators to set goals, develop proper measuring techniques, and provide rewards, then step back as entrepreneurial efforts are implemented to achieve those goals.

We recently established the goal that America's high-school graduates should be the best in the world in math and science achievement. The Reward for Results approach could work beautifully here. Bonuses would be offered to every public school where the average math and science score of the graduating class ties or beats the score of our leading international competitor. The bonuses should be large—say, $5,000 per student. Half would be paid to the school, whereas the half would be given to the students themselves to help pay for college or job training. There are tremendous wealth discrepancies among our nation's schools: Classes in Mississippi have much lower per-student funding than those in Beverly Hills and New York's affluent Westchester County. The bonuses would be adjusted to help compensate for this imbalance.

There is evidence that the Rewards for Results approach can work. The state of South Carolina already awards bonuses to schools for improved results. Not by coincidence, the state has raised its average SAT score forty-eight points in just a few years, a faster increase than any other state in the nation. It's time to apply the same principle nationwide.

A program like Rewards for Results will ultimately pay for itself. Each year, high-school dropouts cost the nation some $260 billion—more than the entire Pentagon budget—in lower wages and reduced taxes alone. The increased spending for welfare, health care, and law enforcement is an unknown and probably unknowable additional burden, but clearly it's huge.

One caveat: As with all changes in the education system, we must be patient. Results take time. No parent wants her child to become an educational guinea pig, subject to every new gimmick and fad. Let's not be like the foolish gardener who impatiently kept pulling up his seedlings, wanting to see the roots grow. We need to apply concerted, long-term plans, based on the best research and experience, and allow them time to produce the results our nation needs and our parents demand.

# Schools as Family Centers

S chools must also adopt a larger role in the community. The increasing demands on families, often resulting in both parents entering the workforce, longer hours, and many other pressures, find millions of children being put into day-care centers of dubious quality or simply fending for themselves. Only our public schools are positioned to make a dent in this problem.

Make no mistake, many parents worry constantly about the choices they must make. Jennifer in San Francisco is typical: "There's no after-school care. My kids are just hanging out, getting into trouble. I can't even think at work, always worrying about the kids."

Tamara, who lives in San Francisco, told me that it literally sickens her to have to put her child in day care. She can't afford much—even though she pays more for day care than she pays for rent—so her child is tended in a large group, with little personal attention. Tamara longs to hear her little girl say, "I had fun today, Mommy." But instead, most days are spent just waiting for Mommy to finish work; the children are being warehoused rather than nurtured and loved.

Telling parents to stay at home is no answer; in today's economy, in fact, that's more like a cruel joke. And when women choose to pursue careers, following opportunities they'd have been denied just a few years ago, their choices should be supported, not denigrated.

But the impact to our children and, ultimately, upon our society from the lack of affordable, quality child care is enormous. Welfare reform has exacerbated the crisis. Under the provisions of the 1996 act, thousands of single mothers were forced to find work. Who's taking care of the kids? It's a question that deserves a better answer than a shrug of the shoulders.

When you're about to fight a battle, you have to start by determining what assets you have. One of the key assets every community has in the battle to support our children is a school building. But it's a sadly underused asset. Most schools are shut down at the end of the school day and left empty until the children show up the next morning. And in some communities, depending on the vagaries of population shifts, classroom space is left empty, whereas in other places schools are bursting at the seams.

Let's put our school buildings to work in new ways to meet our new needs. Decades ago, most public schools instituted kindergarten for five-year-olds, who before then had been kept at home. Today, most families take the advantages of kindergarten for granted. And now we know about the incredible development of the child's brain that takes place between birth and age three. Why not get young children into a constructive learning environment as soon as possible?

As the Affton-Lindbergh School example proves, we could get consistently better educational outcomes if we were able to involve children in the public schools at an earlier age. Perhaps the federal government should add funding on a matching basis to help local schools educate, first, four-year-olds, then three-year-olds. Kids would benefit, and their parents, relieved of worries about finding reliable child care, would benefit, too.

After-school programs represent another huge need and, perhaps, another area where the federal government could aid local schools with matching funds. In most communities, where the schools shut down at three o'clock in the afternoon, where do the children go after school? The invariable answer is back to an empty house or apartment—or onto the streets. But it's no longer rational or sensible to let children out of school for the day with no place to go other than someplace to get into trouble. The local school is the safest and, potentially, the most rewarding alternative.

Another idea worth considering is expanding the school year to eleven or even twelve months. Although the long, lazy days of summer provide some of my fondest childhood memories, we need to update the calendar to fit today's reality. A longer school year may well be necessary to meet the educational demands of the twenty-first century. (Think of all the advances in science alone that today's students must master—to say nothing of all the history that's occurred since you and I were kids!) Year-round schooling would also provide another way for schools to help fill the child-care gap by providing a learning environment for kids during summer months.

In areas where an expanded school year is already a reality, it's often done on a flexible basis so that families can choose which months their children will go to school. This allows families to choose whether to expand their children's horizons through summer camps, family travel, volunteer and paid employment, and other traditional summer activities—or to keep them in school. Offering this kind of choice creates a win-win situation for everybody.

The broadest current concept for expanding the community role of schools may be the model developed by a friend of mine, educator James Comer.

"Comer schools" have popped up in several areas around the country. Under this approach, school buildings become learning centers for the whole community. Services are offered to children as young as five, and the facilities are available into the evening to ensure that children continue to have a nurturing, stimulating environment even after the traditional school day is over. In many communities, doctors and nurses are integrated into the school, so that health care services, from immunizations to screening for early detection of medical problems, are widely available. At some of these schools, adult education is offered, ranging from classes in English and other languages to job-training and -retraining classes. Although the focus is on the kids, the school also becomes a key ingredient in the social, economic, and intellectual health of the community.

Taken together, the ideas I've mentioned constitute a major reform in the way we think of public schools and use them to meet the challenges of modern society. The crucial element, I think, is community involvement, including everyone from newborns to senior citizens. Without it, reform will break up in halfway measures, and the institution of public schools will fall into further disrepute. Yet if more and more people assert ownership over our public schools and reinvent them in a new form relevant to people's real lives, they will fulfill again their vital historic role in American life.

## Bringing College Within the Reach of All

Study after study confirms what most Americans know deep down: Higher education is a key to economic success. Wisely, nearly every American family hopes to send its children on to college one day—both for the career benefits higher education affords and for the richer, more interesting existence that extended learning permits.

Unfortunately, too many families find that they simply can't afford to send their children to college. Many who are able to scrape the money together find that they have to forgo other goals, including, sometimes, a safe and secure retirement. And many graduates find themselves saddled with thousands and thousands of dollars of student loans. Hundreds of dollars a month in debt repayments are a heavy load to bear for young people just starting out.

I know how much my education meant to me, not only because of the fascinating and important things I learned but also because my family and I worked hard to send me to college. The extra work my parents took on, the part-time and summer jobs I worked at, and the precious loan our community church provided to bridge the gap between our savings and the annual tuition bill—all these memories reinforce for me in concrete terms the *value* of my education.

The question today is this: How do we put the same invaluable lessons within the reach of more kids?

A dizzying array of programs is offered at federal, state, and local levels: Stafford loans, Pell Grants, Plus loans, and hundreds of others. States like Georgia have innovative programs like the HOPE Scholarship (now adopted at the federal level), which provides resources to students who keep their grades up and stay clear of drugs and alcohol. Many forms of help are available, but keeping track of them isn't easy, even for professionals like guidance counselors.

A current vogue in government—and a good one—is the idea

of creating one-stop shops for citizens: merging programs, agencies, and offices so that citizens can go to one place to find out all the services available, whether they be targeted for people out of work, senior citizens, mothers and babies, or armed forces veterans. We need to do the same thing for families and students looking for help with attending college or training and retraining programs.

We also need to promote saving for college starting the day a child is born. It'll never be easy for most families to save enough. At the St. Louis campus of the University of Missouri, an in-state student will need roughly $46,000 for four years' tuition. (Out-of-state students pay more.) To be able to afford this, parents would have to save $170 every month for eighteen years. That's about $2,000 a year, a sizeable chunk of the average family's income. Of course, many families have two, three, or more children to consider.

There are things government can do to help. One way is to provide savings vehicles for parents that allow for tax-free building of investments. Nothing is more maddening to a parent than to invest in mutual funds for a child's education and then to find out, on April 15, that they owe taxes on dollars they haven't seen. If they want to keep their money working for a child's education, they should be allowed to do so, tax-free, just as with their retirement funds.

The other side of the problem, of course, is the inflation of college costs. They've been growing at close to twice the rate of overall prices. During 1993 and 1994, we had a national debate about the cost of health care. A combination of public anger, economic pressure, and the perceived threat of national health care legislation sent a powerful message to the health care and insurance industries. They heard the warning and found ways to limit the increases in health care costs for a couple of years. It's time for a similar wake-up call for our colleges and universities. If they don't begin reining in costs soon, they will face public outrage and, ultimately, the threat of government action to force change.

# Finding the Money—A New Approach on Taxes

Throughout these pages I've spoken about the dramatic changes our society is undergoing and the serious pressures these changes are exerting on families. I've also spoken about some of the ways we need to adapt to these changes as parents and citizens, as well as some ways our communities should do more to support families. Both private and public initiatives are necessary; in fact, the public efforts are likely to be of small value if they're not nurtured at a grassroots level by the ideas and the daily contributions of thousands and millions of deeply involved citizens.

Still, there's a basic minimum of government support without which little can be accomplished on a national level. Some might assume that public programs like those I've described are impossible—particularly today, when a generation of Republican leaders has trained voters to reflexively demand tax cuts and "smaller government"—no matter what needs go unmet. Political realism demands that any politician who advocates an active, supportive federal government also have a sensible plan for paying for it.

Everyone hates paying taxes. I'm no exception. But like the vast majority of Americans, I find myself sitting dutifully at the kitchen table as each April 15 approaches, adding columns of figures and filling in those crazy forms. For all our griping about taxes, we Americans boast the highest rate of voluntary tax participation of any industrialized country. It's a real tribute to our democracy and to the strong sense of citizenship that nearly all Americans still share deep in our hearts.

Nonetheless, it must be admitted that our government doesn't make it easy for citizens to do the right thing on tax day. Like more and more people, I now find it necessary to pay someone to help me fill out my forms, although I served for twelve years on the House Ways and Means Committee—the committee that actually *writes* the tax laws! Right now, more than $225 billion and 5.3 billion hours per year are spent on tax filing, tax preparation, and complicated strategies for tax avoidance. It's a huge waste of time and money.

Most people are willing to pay their fair share, but they resent having to engage in acrobatics simply to pay their taxes. And when they see how a few people are able to use gimmicks and loopholes to pay little or no taxes, they find it downright infuriating. As well they should.

I've invested a lot of my political capital in tax reform. One of the earliest campaign statements I made when I first ran for Congress in 1976 called for comprehensive tax reform. Once elected, I spent a great deal of time and energy on the issue. In 1982, I teamed up with Bill Bradley—who represented New Jersey in the Senate at that time, although he actually grew up in what is now my congressional district in Missouri—to introduce a comprehensive bill we dubbed the Fair Tax Act. It would form the basis of the major tax-reform bill that was enacted four years later.

The 1986 Tax Reform Act made some progress, but not enough. And soon after it was passed, the lobbyists set to work, as usual, promoting breaks and special provisions for their favored industries. As a result, the tax code is so riddled with gimmicks, gewgaws, and loopholes that it seriously undermines the relationship between citizens and their government. When the system of defraying the cost of government is unfair—when people's confidence in that system is in question—it can't help but fray the fabric of our country.

I've come to believe it's time to join the Republicans in their call to scrap the tax code and start over. It's a radical notion, but piecemeal approaches just won't work any longer. Unlike many Republicans, however, I'm unwilling to exploit public anger by simply attacking the existing code. Our citizens deserve to know that we also have a realistic plan for replacing it—after all, it's their money.

I've authored a plan that I think can solve the problem. I call it the 10% Tax Plan. It's really simple: Roughly three out of four taxpayers would end up paying no more than 10 percent of their income in federal income taxes. In addition, the other tax rates found in today's code would be lowered dramatically. My plan would reduce the tax burden for 62 percent of U.S. taxpayers—not just those at the top of the ladder, like some of the Republican plans we've seen floated. For everybody from the clerk at the neighborhood hardware store to the CEO of a Silicon Valley software company, rates would drop by as much as one-third.

Under the 10% Tax Plan, a family of four would pay no federal income tax on its first $27,500 in income and no more than a 10-percent rate on income up to $61,000. It's possible to do this, because my plan puts everyone on a level playing field, eliminating the current situation in which those who play by the rules and don't get to take advantage of every preference and loophole have been subsidizing a fortunate few.

By eliminating most tax preferences, we'll dramatically simplify the tax code. A majority of taxpayers could actually choose not to file an income tax form at all through an enhanced system of voluntary withholding. And those who do file a tax form would find it no larger than an ordinary postcard.

The 10% Tax Plan would retain tax breaks for home ownership and health care coverage. Home ownership is a part of the American dream that we should continue to encourage. It's also a tremendous generator of jobs and economic growth in this country, as homeowners buy everything from paint, nails, and lumber to refrigerators, furniture, and the like.

And health care coverage, as I've already discussed, is vital. We should do anything we can do to make health coverage of individuals and families more generally affordable—hence the two tax breaks we'd keep under my plan.

I'd treat all income the same, whether it is earned by the sweat of your brow, the power of your mind, or the sale of your investments. We need to eliminate the myriad preferences in the tax code and give citizens back the power to determine how to conduct their own financial affairs based on what's right for them, not because of tax breaks. However, my plan would allow increases in the value of investments in retirement plans and education accounts that are currently exempt from taxes to remain so. To do otherwise would undermine the very goals I've outlined throughout this book.

Much of what I've written here has been devoted to explaining the complexities and stresses of our new economic environment. It's absurd that our system of financing government should be compounding those complexities. We ought to be helping people regain control of their own economic futures—and taxes are an obvious place to start.

## Taxes and Citizenship

The 10% Tax Plan also includes an important feature that will help guarantee the benefits of tax reform in the future. It's a proposal for a national advisory referendum—a vote by all the citizens—before federal income tax rates can rise again. This amounts to a promise that Congress, if real tax reform indeed becomes reality, won't be able to turn around and undermine the integrity of the new system.

This provision of my tax-reform plan has received more attention from some of my closest political friends than almost any other. Some have warned me to reconsider it. "Think about where this may lead," they say. "If we have to conduct a national advisory referendum on tax rates, what's to stop the public from demanding similar referendums on school vouchers, defense spending, abortion, gun control, or any other issue? Where will it all end?"

I've thought long and hard about this proposal. It's not a brand-new idea; in fact, I introduced national advisory referendum legislation in Congress as far back as the 1980s. I believe that we need to get our citizens more interested and involved in running their country, and giving them final say over a handful of crucial issues is a sensible way of doing this.

Why start with the tax system? Because taxes are a key link between individuals and their government—so much so that I believe we need to look at this issue differently from others. And confidence in the tax system has been so deeply undermined by years of political game-playing that I think we need something as dramatic as a referendum to show clearly that we are putting the tax laws back in the hands of all the people.

Are there risks in this referendum idea? Yes. The referendum process has been abused in some states by special interests preying on the public. Last year, for example, business interests in California spent millions of dollars promoting a referendum to limit the ability of average working people to participate in the political process through their unions. With the help of a sophisticated—and highly misleading—media campaign, they gained significant public support for their proposal. Only after a concerted counter-attack by labor and citizens' groups did the public discover what was really at stake. On election day, the business initiative was defeated.

We don't want to create a new battleground for special interests at the national level. Therefore, I'd favor limiting the number and scope of issues that could be subject to a referendum—perhaps, in fact, making only the tax issue subject to such a vote. But it's a debate I think we need to have, a debate that would be healthy for the country.

I don't believe our problems as a nation are caused by too much citizen involvement—just the opposite. And reversing that trend by putting more power into the hands of ordinary Americans is important enough to justify taking a few risks. Our democracy deserves no less.

# III

# Beyond the Politics
# of Destruction

A RENEWED IDEAL OF CITIZENSHIP

# "Just Get 'Em to the Polls!"

Like most Americans of my generation, I first learned about democracy and citizenship while in school. What surprises me, looking back, is how uniformly, unabashedly patriotic the message was. When I was in grade school and high school in St. Louis, and even later, in college and law school—when you might have thought a bit of cynicism would have crept in—my teachers always talked about politics and public service in glowing terms, as a responsibility of all citizens, especially those fortunate enough to get a good education. The implication was clear: You could certainly use your schooling as a stepping-stone to making a lot of money, but it would be far nobler to enter public life to serve the community and the country.

Two political role models especially stood out for me. One was Harry Truman. Like me, he'd come from Missouri, and he'd returned home with his wife, Bess, to Independence in 1952 after completing his term as president. When I was growing up, Truman wasn't generally considered one of our greatest presidents—his reputation has risen in recent years—but there was no denying he was a frank, feisty, incorruptible character whose honesty people couldn't help liking.

Then there was John F. Kennedy, who was president when I was in college. It was exciting to have a president so youthful, so talented, and so richly endowed with personal gifts—wit, charm, and intelligence, to say nothing of a beautiful wife—working so hard on behalf of the country. If someone so gifted could forgo making money in favor of devoting his best years to public service, then surely others—even people far less talented, like me—could and should do the same.

Neither of my parents was active in politics. They voted in every election and were very patriotic, but they never ran for office or volunteered to help in a campaign. Nonetheless, the political bug bit me early. When I was a kid, we usually had relatives at the house for Sunday dinner. Unlike the typical kid, I always hung around to listen when the grown-ups' talk over coffee turned to politics. I read everything I could find about politics and watched political shows on television whenever I could. I developed the habit of running out to the front lawn first thing in the morning to fetch that day's *Globe-Democrat* so I could read the latest news about sports—especially St. Louis Cardinals baseball—and about local and national politics.

One summer, when I was visiting my aunt and uncle in Oklahoma, I spent an entire week watching the Democratic National Convention on TV. (In those days, the networks would broadcast the conventions gavel to gavel, as if the politicos' oratory, arguments, demonstrations, and other quadrennial antics were essential business for everyone—as I think they are, in fact.) My aunt started calling me "Hothouse Rose" because I stayed in the house all week, eyes glued to the TV set, while my cousins were outside playing. I guess it must have been the 1952 convention, in Chicago, which nominated Illinois favorite son Adlai Stevenson for his first run at the presidency; I would have been eleven years old at the time.

I dabbled in politics a little myself in college. I ran for vice president of my freshman class at Northwestern and won. Later, I was elected president of the student senate and of my fraternity. But it wasn't until I returned home to St. Louis after earning my law degree at the University of Michigan that I began a real involvement in politics.

Almost immediately after settling in at home, Jane and I went to a local Democratic ward meeting, eager to find out what we could do to help the party. (Jane has always been my partner in life, in every sense of the word; there are very few things we care about that we haven't shared. When it comes to politics, I was probably the one with the real passion, but Jane was interested, too, and she's been there with me every step of the way. As you can probably tell, I'm a very lucky guy.) The meeting was held in the basement of an American Legion Hall, the true smoke-filled room of proverb. We sat through the meeting, only a portion of which we understood, waiting until we could get to meet and talk to Phelim O'Toole, the ward committeeman and clerk of the circuit court. Phelim was an elderly Irish curmudgeon, wheelchair-bound from a bad case of arthritis.

When Jane and I introduced ourselves to Phelim, he eyed us suspiciously. It was obvious, even to us greenhorns, that most of the members of the ward organization were city employees who'd come to the meeting only because it was an unwritten job requirement. Jane and I, a couple of young, bright-eyed idealists, didn't exactly blend into the group. Frankly, no one was very happy to see us; I'm sure they wondered who the heck we were and why we were interested in politics.

(Years later, a fellow congressman, Abner Mikva of Illinois, told me about his own first ward meeting in Chicago. When Abner walked in, fresh out of law school, the committeeman's first question was, "Who sent you?" Abner replied, "No one sent me. I want to volunteer." "Fine, fine," the committeeman responded, "But *who sent you?*" Puzzled, Abner persisted, "You don't understand! No one sent me—I'm a volunteer!" The committeeman shrugged and dismissed Abner with the comment, "We don't want nobody nobody sent!")

Nevertheless, after asking us a few questions to establish our bona fides, Phelim asked us if we wanted to be precinct captains. Of course, we agreed. "All right, then," he said. "Here's what you do. I want you to go door to door, to every house in the 2nd precinct in St. Louis. You've gotta meet every single Democrat in the whole precinct—understand? Then, when election day comes around, you're gonna stand at the polls and check off every Democrat who comes to vote. Get the idea?"

"Sure," I said. "But what if some of them don't show up?"

"If it gets to be five o'clock at night, and some of the Democrats haven't voted yet, you gotta go and *get* them. Pick 'em up in your car, carry 'em on your back, I don't care—just get 'em to the polls, understand?" This was our introduction to the nuts and bolts of party politics—a side of politics we hadn't learned much about in civics class.

Jane and I did as we were told. On every election day, we stood at the polling place and made sure "our" Democrats actually voted. Many times I drove our family car to the homes of voters, especially elderly ones, and personally escorted them to the polls. Between elections, we went to every ward meeting and got to know the other precinct captains; many became good friends. Although most of them didn't relish the "volunteer" work they had to do to keep their jobs at the courthouse or in City Hall, they did enjoy the social side of politics, and we had a lot of fun with some of them.

I was surprised and disappointed to discover that few ordinary citizens came to the ward meetings or otherwise participated in politics. I was also disappointed to find out that the committeeman and committeewoman endorsed Democratic candidates for office based mainly on how much money they'd contributed to the ward organization. My idealism was somewhat restored when I saw the favored candidates lose our ward, despite the official endorsement, to candidates who were more popular and ran a better television campaign. (Reflecting on the role of television in more recent elections, I'm no longer sure I feel the same way. One thing is certain: Those early days in my political life look like an innocent time compared to today.)

## "Young Man, You're an Alderman!"

In 1968—that tumultuous year in national politics—Phelim O'Toole, my first political mentor, died. Soon thereafter, committeewoman Margaret Butler offered to appoint me as his replacement until the next election. I happily accepted, as I was hoping to run for alderman someday. (Our Democratic alderman had been defeated by a Republican just one year earlier.) A stint as committeeman would help position me for that race, I thought.

In 1970, Stuart Symington was running for his fourth term in the U.S. Senate. A former business executive and a member of President Truman's cabinet, he'd become a moderately liberal senator who'd vied for the presidential nomination in 1956; now, in 1970, he was one of the more dovish senators in regard to the Vietnam War. I volunteered to help on Symington's campaign. One thing led to another, and by the late summer I was so involved that I was asked to take a leave from my law firm to work full-time for the campaign for the last three months. I did that, and I learned a lot about the details of running a campaign—planning public appearances, preparing ads and leaflets, organizing rallies, dealing with the press, and much more. Symington won a narrow reelection victory over state Attorney General John Danforth, whether despite my help or because of it I've never known.

In January 1971, soon after the Symington campaign ended, I filed papers declaring my intention to run for alderman for the 14th ward in the city of St. Louis—my own first real campaign. I made plans to hit the ground running by going door to door throughout the district, starting the very first weekend after I filed. Unfortunately, a blizzard that weekend blanketed the Midwest. I didn't let that stop me, although I know I must have looked silly, tromping through the drifts with my snow hat pulled down over my head. However, the experience convinced me that door-to-door canvassing was the best way to campaign, because so many people that day told me, "If you're out on a day like this, I'm going to vote for you." (Maybe they were just too polite to say what they were really thinking: "If you're *crazy enough* to be out on a day like this . . . ")

In the end, I visited every house in the ward at least once, some houses twice. Jane and my parents often accompanied me, and Jane and I printed campaign flyers on a hand-cranked mimeo machine in our basement. Even Bonnie, our Labrador retriever, got into the act. The lady who lived in the house behind ours knitted

Bonnie a coat emblazoned with the slogan "GO FOR GEP." Bonnie became an informal mascot, accompanying us to campaign picnics and during our door-to-door travels. We knew we had to invest every possible ounce of energy into the race; I was running against a popular Republican alderman, and we knew it was going to be a tight contest.

On election night, we watched the votes come in at ward headquarters. With all the precincts in but one, we were in a virtual tie. Ferd Kaufman, one of the clerks in the courthouse, was the Democratic precinct captain for the precinct that was still outstanding, and I stood on the street outside our storefront headquarters waiting—for hours, it seemed—for Ferd to bring the vote totals from that final precinct. Finally, I saw Ferd walking down the sidewalk—a big, burly man with a mustache and a gruff manner. As he approached, I could see that he had a big scowl on his face, and my heart sank. Ferd got right up to me, grabbed and hugged me, then shouted: "Young man, you're an alderman!" I was elated. I had won by 112 votes!

I'd been a door-to-door candidate, and now I wanted to be a door-to-door alderman. Although the campaign was over, I continued to visit homes throughout the district in order to keep in touch with the "customers." It's amazing how much more candid voters are with you, alone on their doorstep, than when they see you in a public setting. Not only do they have a chance to communicate directly and personally with someone who represents them in government, but you're on their turf, a factor that makes constituents much more comfortable about sharing real problems, worries, grievances, and dreams.

I continued my door-to-door work consistently through five years as an alderman and now twenty-two years as a congressman.

During my last two campaigns, I also spent ten to twelve hours each day wearing a telephone headset to speak with undecided voters. One of the powerful lessons successful businesses have learned in recent years is the importance of constant, close communication with customers, and I try to apply this lesson to my work in politics. Government in general doesn't do enough of this. Too often, it operates like a big, self-satisfied business that believes it can get by with shoddy and indifferent service. Lots of once-proud companies that fell prey to this attitude have failed, and the same problem underlies much of the public's current disdain for government.

## Politics Is a Service Business

E arly in my political career, I had the benefit of sage advice from two older, successful politicians. During the first days of my tenure on the Board of Aldermen, "Red" Villa, the dean of the board (and the owner of a popular south St. Louis saloon), counseled, "Dick, politics never changes. How you do in the next election depends on how well you've responded to what the voters need. They're going to look at whether you got their tree trimmed, the pothole on their street fixed, or the dead dog picked up from the alley behind their house—not how you voted on the city budget."

"Never forget," Red told me, "you're in a service business. If you fail to give the customer what he wants, you'll soon be out of business! It's no different from my saloon. If the beer glasses in my place are dirty one day, it's no big deal. But if they're dirty two days in a row, the customers'll go to the saloon on the next corner—if it has clean glasses." Red didn't have a fancy education, but he well understood some fundamental truths about business, human nature, and politics.

The second politician who helped me was Tip O'Neill, Speaker of the House when I first joined Congress in 1977. His advice to all new members was simple, and today it is one of our best-known aphorisms: "All politics is local." In a way, Tip was saying the same thing Red Villa had said, though as a national leader. What really matters to people is what is physically in front of them—their neighborhoods, their schools, their parks, the post office and Social Security office two blocks down the street. If "government" is only an abstraction to people, it is worthless to them, but if it is seen as effectively addressing real problems in their everyday lives, it will be considered worthwhile and valuable.

Here's a story that illustrates this point vividly. In 1993, the Great Flood of the Mississippi River devastated wide stretches of America's Midwest, including my home district in Missouri. It happened to be a busy time on Capitol Hill, with many crucial issues coming up for votes. And although I had to be in Washington during the week, the seriousness of the situation at home dictated that I return to Missouri as often as possible during the flood and its aftermath to help my constituents. Some weeks, this called for two or three round-trips between St. Louis and Washington.

The effects of the flood were appalling. Hundreds of homes and businesses were under water in my district alone, and thousands of people were homeless. There was plenty to do. I helped coordinate local, state, and federal flood-relief efforts and toured the devastated areas by helicopter and boat to assess the problems and to help rescue people and animals. I visited volunteer sites to help fill sandbags, to serve hot meals, and to thank and urge on the volunteers who came to help us from all over the country.

Two years later, voters in my district were asked in a poll what they remembered about my service in the Congress, which now spanned almost twenty years. For many of those years, I'd been among the House leadership, deeply involved in such high-profile issues as the federal budget deficit, Social Security, trade regulations, and many others. I'd also had a big hand in bringing important and valuable public-works projects to my district. Nevertheless, in the poll, my constituents said the only thing they could recall about my years in Congress was my work at home during the Great Flood of 1993.

Red Villa and Tip O'Neill knew what they were talking about.

## The Education of a Young Turk

While serving on the Board of Aldermen, I worked closely with four other young aldermen, and our group became known as the "Young Turks." We were very aggressive about wanting to shore up and revitalize the neighborhoods of St. Louis, which were experiencing many of the problems common to urban America during the early 1970s. Many neighborhoods had fallen into disrepair as the relatively well-to-do fled for the suburbs, leaving the city as a repository for the aged and the poor. The Young Turks became a force of five seeking to pull together citizen efforts to reverse these trends.

One of the things I did was to draw up the legal papers to form four or five neighborhood corporations, devoted to such purposes as neighborhood property improvement, law enforcement, programs for kids and the elderly, and other revitalization efforts. We also launched neighborhood festivals, featuring local and ethnic foods, music and dancing, arts and crafts, and other fun activities. The festivals served several purposes: They were fund-raising events for neighborhood improvement efforts; they allowed the local people to show off the best aspects of their neighborhoods to people from outside; and they also provided a nifty excuse for residents to fix up their properties for festival day.

I also helped launch two citizen efforts to improve life in the neighborhoods in my ward. The first was a cleanup program. I wrote letters to everyone in a particular neighborhood, telling them I'd be coming through their streets on a particular Saturday with a big truck to pick up large items of trash—old refrigerators, lumber, piles of bricks, you name it. I'd also announce an alley sweep and cleanup for the same day, asking for volunteers from each block. The combined effort really changed the psychology of the neighborhood, getting many people actively participating in improvements that made a positive difference in the look of the community.

The second effort was a neighborhood watch program in which we asked citizens to ride through their neighborhoods at night, looking out for criminal activity. We operated this program in conjunction with the police department, whose eyes and ears our citizen-volunteers became.

Both of these efforts brought together private, voluntary citizen efforts with government help to solve community problems. (For neighborhood cleanup day, for example, we had arranged with the sanitation department to borrow a garbage truck and to leave the refuse we collected at the city dump.) Both efforts recognized two obvious truths: The people cannot solve all their problems alone, and neither can the government. But when individual citizens do their part while the government is doing its part, real progress can be made.

These experiences simultaneously reflected and shaped my developing political philosophy. I developed a healthy skepticism about both the dogma of the left—that government is the answer to everything—and the dogma of the right—that government can do nothing right. The correct answer is that both individuals and government must share efforts to solve community and family problems.

As an alderman, I also learned that you can accomplish a lot if you throw yourself into community service for the sake of the goals you're trying to achieve rather than personal or political credit. As Ronald Reagan used to say, you can get a lot done in Washington as long as you don't care who gets the credit. I learned that lesson early as a St. Louis alderman.

Red Villa once told me, "Kid, remember—you only got your word and your vote. Guard both, because once you commit either, you *have* to do what you say you will do. Once you lose your credibility with your colleagues or your voters, you might as well leave."

I never forgot what he told me. It was a fundamental lesson of politics and life—that trust is the essential foundation of human relationships.

To nurture that trust, I soon discovered, mutual respect and civility were crucial ingredients in every relationship, whether among the legislators or between the legislators and the citizens. The greater the emotional impact of an issue, the more important simple decency became. At zoning hearings, for example, tempers would often run high on the part of citizens and legislators alike, perhaps because pocketbook issues like the value of someone's home or business were usually involved. When this happened, I often found myself playing the role of peacemaker. I'd try to calm a tense situation by reminding everyone that we had to respect everyone's opinion and their right to express themselves. That simple admonition would usually make it possible for the meeting to continue peacefully.

When I was elected to Congress in 1976, I found that most of the simple lessons I'd learned while serving on the St. Louis Board of Aldermen were equally applicable. For example, Dick Bolling, a U.S. representative from Kansas City, Missouri, was my mentor, and he said the same things Red Villa had said about the sacredness of my word and my vote. The arena was greater, the issues more momentous, the public spotlight more glaring, but the same principles—including the "localness" of politics—remained in force.

# The People's House

"Contempt of Congress" is supposed to be a crime, but it's also a long American tradition. No less a figure than Mark Twain once wrote, "It could probably be shown by facts and figures that there is no distinctly native American criminal class except Congress." I don't suppose our reputation could have sunk much lower in the years since.

Truth is, what's amazing is not how little good Congress does. It's amazing how *much* we manage to accomplish. When people gripe about how ineffective Congress is, I sometimes ask, "Have you ever served on a committee? How many members did it have?"

They usually reply, "Oh, eight or twelve."

"And was it easy to make decisions?"

The usual answer: "No way! We fought for hours."

"Well," I respond, "Imagine being a member of a committee of 535 people!" That's how many men and women we have in Congress, including both the House and the Senate—535 strong-willed individuals of every race, creed, age, gender, occupation, and political philosophy. I'm amazed that we get *anything* done!

The Founders designed the United States Congress to be a true representation of the nation in all its diversity. It remains so to this day, which is one of the main reasons I love it so. And if at times its sheer size makes its deliberations seem agonizingly slow, even this serves a useful purpose. It allows maximum input from all our citizens—from the lobbyists and "impartial experts" who besiege us daily to the thousands of ordinary folks who call, email, and send handwritten letters advocating their favorite causes. The process is so open to citizen involvement that when a resolution to a particular issue is finally reached even the losers are almost always willing to accept the decision. They sense, at the very least, that their voices have been heard.

This is no mean feat; the single great rupture in our nation's history, the Civil War, occurred when the political leaders of certain states, unwilling to accept the verdict of the majority, decided to jump ship. Keeping our vast and populous nation moving together as one—despite the constant stresses and strains of disagreement—is a little-noticed but absolutely remarkable achievement, for which our unwieldy yet all-embracing Congress deserves much of the credit.

Earlier in this book I wrote about the debate over NAFTA, the

North American Free Trade Agreement. It was one of the most contentious issues I've ever seen on the House floor. For weeks, people around the nation debated the merits of the treaty, and groups having a special interest in the outcome—with business leaders backing NAFTA, labor organizations opposing it—worked overtime in search of public and congressional support.

After a long and heartfelt debate on the floor of the House, with many eloquent and well-reasoned statements on both sides of the issue, NAFTA finally passed. I was deeply disappointed. But what impressed me most was the reaction I encountered in the weeks and months that followed, when I traveled the country, meeting with union leaders and groups of workers who'd fought bitterly against the treaty. They were discouraged, yes. But they all expressed their willingness to try to make the treaty work to benefit both the United States and Mexico—and, if they could, to amend it later through peaceful, legal means.

Everyone understood, as if instinctively, that this is how democracy works. The nation engages in a robust debate; all voices are heard; and our duly elected representatives cast their votes. The result inevitably pleases some and displeases others, but in the end we close ranks, one nation after all.

Two other historic votes stand out in my recollection as exemplifying the greatness of which Congress, at its best, is capable.

When the armies of Iraq's Saddam Hussein invaded Kuwait in 1990, the world reacted with outrage. President George Bush declared, "This shall not stand," and he made clear that the United States was prepared to lead a military action to force an Iraqi withdrawal. As Majority Leader in the House of Representatives, I was involved with other congressional leaders from both parties in a series of White House meetings with the president, Chairman of the Joint Chiefs of Staff Colin Powell, and Secretary of State James Baker to discuss the developing crisis.

As a team of American diplomats visited capitals around the world, seeking international support for a military response, President Bush ordered a half-million U.S. troops into the Persian Gulf region, hoping their presence would convince Saddam to back down. At this point, with the world poised between peace and war, some of my House colleagues began agitating for a congressional declaration of war before any further military action was taken.

I, too, felt strongly that we should not put our military men and women in harm's way without an authorizing vote by the Congress. The Constitution clearly states that only the Congress has the power to declare war (although many presidents have engaged in military action without congressional authorization, relying on their constitutionally prescribed role as commander in chief of the armed forces). I knew well the damage done both to our nation and to our system of checks and balances when we became embroiled in a protracted, costly conflict in Vietnam with no formal declaration of war. A congressional vote to legitimize presidential action in the Gulf, I felt, would do much to unite the nation behind our military; and if war against Iraq was a mistake, a debate in Congress might give us a chance to recognize that fact in time. Either way, honoring the declaration of war procedure as provided in the Constitution would serve our nation's interests.

At almost every White House meeting, I spoke up, urging President Bush to ask for congressional authorization before going to war against Iraq. His response was silence. Later, we learned that the president had been troubled by doubts that he could win a vote in Congress and that he was bound and determined to go ahead with an invasion whether or not Congress approved. Finally, under intense pressure—and perhaps having concluded that he could win the vote after all—the president agreed to present the issue to Congress.

For two days in January 1991, we debated the authorization motion, knowing that armed forces from the United States and an array of allies were poised to take the offensive in Kuwait and Iraq at any time. As millions watched on C-SPAN, almost every member of the House rose in turn to speak, and the outpouring of serious, thoughtful, historically informed arguments on both sides was truly impressive. Emotions were high, yet civility and mutual respect were the order of the day, as if the knowledge that we held in our hands the lives of thousands of Americans and many more from other nations induced a sense of sober nonpartisanship.

In a close vote, the motion to invade passed. And immediately thereafter, we also passed a unanimous resolution declaring that the Congress fully supported our troops in their mission to expel the Iraqis from Kuwait. We'd reached agreement on behalf of 260 million Americans.

I hate to think of the second-guessing that would have resulted had the president launched an invasion without the consent of the Congress—particularly if the war that followed had proven to be lengthy or unsuccessful.

Which takes me to a final story, this one concerning another watershed event in recent American history—President Clinton's 1993 budget.

Starting in 1981, the federal government ran huge budget deficits for a full decade. President Ronald Reagan was making the argument that huge tax cuts would so stimulate economic growth that no deficits would result. Like many, I was skeptical; and sure enough, by the late 1980s we were running deficits that exceeded $200 billion each year. By 1992, the national debt was more than $4 trillion—more than five times what it had been when I joined Congress in 1977.

When I met with newly elected President Bill Clinton in Little Rock, Arkansas, during November 1992, I told him his greatest challenge was to tackle the huge and growing deficit: "Dealing honestly with the budget deficit is the ticket that will let us play in the game to fix the rest of what needs to be fixed in the economy." The president agreed and promised to do just that.

Some months later, President Clinton's 1993 budget plan came to the floor of the House. As I'd hoped, it honestly addressed the deficit problem. That meant it was filled with political pain. Giving out tax cuts is like handing out candy bars to the voters; ordering tax increases and spending cuts is more like serving spinach. People may know it's good for them, but very few are genuinely enthusiastic.

To make matters worse, then–Minority Whip Newt Gingrich had warned me after the election that we would not get one Republican vote for the president's budget. He said, "You got elected—you find the votes." I was chagrined, but it was the political reality.

On the day we'd scheduled the vote, after an intense period of lobbying on all fronts, our Democratic task force was still furiously working to find the votes we needed to pass the budget. At four o'-clock in the afternoon, Speaker of the House Tom Foley called me to ask if we had the votes. "I don't know," I told him, "and we won't know until the vote is taken, so we might as well go ahead."

I went up to the floor with a sense of dread. I didn't know what was going to happen—I knew we could easily lose—and I knew the outcome was very important to the future of our country. Another such opportunity to free ourselves from the crushing burden of debt might not arise for a long, long time.

On the floor, I continued working on undecided members, even as the actual vote began. Members of Congress usually vote using electronic devices; a running tally appears on the two far walls of the chamber, like a digital scoreboard. The process takes some twenty minutes. When the official time for the vote ended, the yeas and nays were in a flat-footed tie—which meant, under congressional rules, that the budget would not pass.

I was standing at that moment with four as-yet undecided Democratic members, begging them to vote for the budget. In the next few minutes, two of them voted for it and two of them voted against it. We were still tied.

Out of the corner of my eye, I saw Marjorie Margolies-Mezvinsky, a Democratic representative from a mainly Republican district in Pennsylvania. I had talked to her earlier, and she'd said she would vote with us if we really needed her vote. True to her word, Marjorie was now going to cast the deciding ballot. She walked up to the desk to register her vote by card instead of by electronic device. When the budget-approving tally flashed on the wall, many of the Republican members stood in their chairs, waving and shouting derisively, "Bye-bye, Marjorie!" Their message was clear: Marjorie would pay for her vote at the next election.

They were right. Marjorie lost her congressional seat in 1994, primarily because of that vote.

I have never been prouder of the House of Representatives—and of my party—than I was on that day. Members like Marjorie Margolies-Mezvinsky voted in the best interests of their constituents, even against their own political interests. Many people think there's no more integrity in politics. They're wrong. This was a clear example of a modern profile in courage, though few people even noticed.

## Elections Have Consequences

*Elections have consequences*—it's a favorite saying of mine. Oddly, many Americans don't seem to believe it. They think—at least according to the pollsters—that it doesn't matter which party controls the Congress or whom we elect to the presidency or any other office. The one strong conviction about party politics that I've seen attributed to the voting public in recent years is a negative one—the idea that the American people want different political parties to control the presidency and the Congress so that neither party holds too much power. If true, it suggests that most voters prefer a government so politically hamstrung that it can do almost nothing. I'm not sure I believe the pollsters on this one, but I do think most Americans have little appreciation for the positive importance of politics in their lives.

To a degree, this is nothing new. We've been a nation of individualists from our earliest frontier days, with a strong libertarian streak—a desire to be left alone by the government. Henry David Thoreau, that cantankerous Yankee philosopher, spoke for something permanent in the American character when he started his essay "Civil Disobedience" with the words, "I heartily accept the motto,—'That government is best which governs least;' and I should like to see it acted up to more rapidly and systematically." Or consider Twain's imperishable characters, Huck Finn and runaway Jim, riding their homemade raft down the Mississippi, answerable to no one. They represent the kind of self-image many Americans still cherish, deep inside.

But there's a paradox: People want government out of their lives until something they take for granted is missing. If the local public school falls short of parents' standards—if a favorite lake or river is fouled by industrial waste—if Mom's nursing home becomes overcrowded or unsafe—Americans will rise up in an effort to turn things around, often demanding government involvement to make things right. We Americans have a long, rich history of not being involved in political action until the need for self-help is obvious; then we have an equally long, equally rich history of swinging into action to solve problems as a community.

That being said, much of what we've accomplished as a nation would have been impossible without a strong government role— that is, without the people acting together, joining forces to do what no one person or small group could achieve. The examples are too numerous even to list here. They range from the way thirteen loosely knit colonies joined forces to free their people from British rule to the exploration of space two centuries later.

Every generation contributes to the story. As I was coming of age, for instance, the GI Bill was helping to fund higher education for a generation of veterans who would fuel our nation's amazing postwar economic boom, while almost simultaneously the creation of the national highway system was making coast-to-coast commerce—and tourism—faster, easier, and more economical than ever. We Americans are an independent lot, to be sure. But we've banded together for the common good in countless inspiring ways.

# "Government Is the Problem"

Today, however, Americans appear to have forgotten much of this history. The positive, creative role of government is rarely mentioned; its flaws and failings constantly are. We ignore the role of Social Security in lifting tens of millions of elderly people out of the poverty that was once their common lot; instead, we cite the poverty that remains as "proof" that government efforts to help the poor are pointless.

The most disturbing trend in America today is our widespread cynicism about politics and government. People think politics is too negative and politicians are entirely self-serving. Of course, there's a grain of truth in this; there are scoundrels among politicians, just as there are in every profession. But the complaints I hear about government aren't always well-founded or even logical.

At a recent forum I attended, one citizen complained, "You people in Congress are spineless, without values—you stand for nothing except what the latest polls say." Others around the room nodded in agreement. Then a second person spoke: "And you never get anything done in Congress, because all you do is argue. Why can't you put aside ideology and figure out how to work together?" Again, many people nodded. No one even seemed to notice that the two complaints were directly contradictory! We've become so unthinkingly antigovernment that we'll agree with *any* attack on politics—even if it makes no sense.

Still, the current revulsion expressed toward government isn't entirely without foundation. Many forces have combined to drive citizen apathy and negativism to all-time highs. I've already alluded to some of them; others, perhaps, deserve further discussion.

First, as I said before, government hasn't always been very efficient or solicitous of the needs and interests of its customers—the citizens. In fact, the very idea that those receiving government services ought to be thought of as customers, deserving the rights and respect that any customer demands, is relatively new. That's our fault, and it's a good thing we're finally moving to address it through programs like the Taxpayer's Bill of Rights, the reinventing government initiatives, and other ongoing efforts to downsize, streamline, and simplify government. These things should have been done long ago.

However, most of the other forces contributing to the disrepute in which government is held are external ones, some of them deliberately manipulated by those who hope to gain from them. For example, one of our major political parties—the Republican Party—has run its campaigns for the last two decades mainly on the premise that government doesn't solve people's problems but is *itself* the problem (whatever that means). Let's ignore the question why people who despise government are apparently so eager to be elected to government jobs. Let's simply ask the following: Isn't it the height of cynicism for Republican strategists to deliberately foster an attitude of contempt for government as a means of grabbing government power?

It's an ultimately self-defeating strategy as well. One day, a Republican administration, facing some dire national emergency, may need to draw on the wells of public patriotism and idealism in order to save the country—only to find that those wells are empty, having been drained by decades of Republican mockery of government.

# Why Now?

Earlier in this book, I spoke about the "cycle of destruction"—the downward spiral of attack and counterattack in which our political life has been trapped for some twenty-five years. It began, I think, with Watergate and has culminated—at least for now—with the Clinton impeachment. Each new stage in this cycle of violence has further eroded our national sense of citizenship—the recognition, by average citizens, of the value and importance of political life and their willingness to participate and contribute to that life.

As a congressman, I've been able to witness personally how the tactics of personal attack and ethical accusation were used in a deliberate and calculated way as part of a bid for power by one of the leading practitioners of the politics of destruction, Newt Gingrich of Georgia. While he was a backbencher in Congress, Gingrich devoted two years to personally investigating charges of wrongdoing by the Speaker of the House, Democrat Jim Wright. (He said the research was as grueling and extensive as writing a Ph.D. thesis—and Gingrich, a sometime college professor, knows exactly what he's talking about.)

Gingrich managed to dig up some accusations that stuck, involving excessive royalty payments on a book that Wright wrote and sold to groups that supported him politically. Under pressure, Wright finally resigned, and Congressman Tony Coelho was dragged down in the undertow—he too resigned when he thought he was about to be hauled before the Ethics Committee for allegedly improper stock-trading practices.

As one might expect, these Republican assaults did not go

unanswered. After the Republicans won a majority in the House in 1994, Democrats launched an ethics investigation of their own, probing various political practices of Newt Gingrich, including the sale of tapes of a college history course that were a thinly disguised Republican fundraising effort. This investigation ended in a formal reprimand of Gingrich by the full House and a $300,000 fine.

I didn't instigate or support the charges against Gingrich. I was already weary and disgusted with the pattern of attack and counterattack, appalled by the erosion of collegiality in the House I'd long served. But as some of my Democratic colleagues continued their counteroffensive against Republicans, I was briefly caught in the cross fire.

During the investigation of Gingrich, I was warned to call off the "dogs" (as if I could), with the warning that I'd be sorry if I didn't. My enemies tried to make good on their threat. A few weeks later, a right-wing magazine in Washington ran an exposé on Gephardt's "Million Dollar House on the Outer Banks of North Carolina," questioning how I had been able to afford such a home on a congressman's salary. Most of the facts were wrong, and those that were right were artfully shaded for effect, but the inevitable ethics charge was soon brought against me by a Republican member of the leadership. Other stories followed in the mainstream press.

The year-long investigation by the Ethics Committee into this partisan brouhaha wound up with a dismissal of all charges against me. Meanwhile, a number of other members of the Democratic House leadership had ethics charges filed against them by Republican members in a clear tit-for-tat pattern of retaliation for the charges against Gingrich. Ultimately, all were dismissed.

Personal attacks, of course, are not new to politics. Abraham Lincoln was called a "gorilla" by his enemies; Franklin D. Roosevelt was attacked as a communist and a traitor; and the tirades and unsubstantiated charges launched by Senator Joseph McCarthy during the 1950s have made his name a byword for smearing and intimidation. When fair political means have failed, the most passionate advocates are always tempted to reach for the foul.

But I can't find in our political history *any* cycle of destruction as sustained as the one we've witnessed during the past twenty-five years. Both parties have gone on the attack; men and women, peaceful and tolerant by nature, have been dragged into the fray. And others beyond the politicians themselves have gotten involved. We have citizens ranging from James Carville and Alan Dershowitz to Geraldo Rivera and Larry Flynt doing battle on the airwaves in support of President Clinton, whereas William Bennett, Richard Mellon Scaife, Pat Robertson, and Jerry Falwell line up against him. As the stakes grow higher, more and more talented and able citizens choose up sides in the war to save their cause and their hero.

What has changed in America to transform our political life in this way? I believe there are several factors at work.

First, television has affected politics even more profoundly than we realize. The depth of this change was brought home to me during the 1980 presidential campaign. I had the chance to watch one of the televised debates between President Jimmy Carter and his Republican challenger, Ronald Reagan, while in the company of a group of Democratic precinct captains from the congressional district I represent in Missouri. When the debate was over, I was pleased; I thought Carter had really thumped Reagan on the issues, appearing far more knowledgeable and informed. But when

I said as much to my Democratic friends, they shook their heads. To a person, each one agreed that Reagan had won the debate. Stunned, I asked why. Their answer stunned me still more: "We don't know why, we just *like* Reagan better than Carter."

I didn't realize it at the time, but that night I was witnessing firsthand the monumental change that television has brought to politics. Citizens—even active, well-informed citizens—now vote for the politicians they *like*. They no longer choose candidates simply because of their stands on the issues, their vision of America, or their plans for our future; instead, voters increasingly make choices based on how they feel in their guts about the candidates as human beings.

Well into our own century, voters rarely saw or heard presidential candidates. They based their votes upon party affiliations or upon information from newspaper accounts, printed records of debates, and political broadsides. Today, everyone can see and hear politicians on television. Voters can make human judgments about politicians as people, much the same way they decide whether they like Jerry Seinfeld, Barbara Walters, Jay Leno, or any other televised personality.

Campaign tactics have evolved accordingly. TV advertising for candidates focuses on images rather than issues. And when positive imagery about your own candidate proves insufficient, negative ads about your opponent are the only alternative. As was demonstrated by Michael Dukakis's 1988 presidential campaign, when attacked a candidate must counterattack quickly. A cycle of charge and countercharge becomes the inevitable pattern of most political campaigns. If you fail to answer constant attacks, then you lose.

To provide fodder for the assault on one's opponent, negative research is now a necessity. Any scandal or embarrassment that can be dug up—no matter how dated, irrelevant, or distorted—is saved for use at the most opportune moment. Government mechanisms, like independent counsels and ethics committees, can be manipulated to help generate, publicize, and promote such charges. And the media, of course, serve as a powerful accomplice.

The media world in which today's journalists operate has also changed dramatically in ways that help foster the politics of destruction. With more television networks and cable channels than ever, not to mention the burgeoning universe of the Internet, there are many, many more outlets for information than there were a generation ago. As such outlets have proliferated, competition among journalists has increased proportionately.

Furthermore, the media today are more driven by the desire for commercial success than at any time during our past, due in part to changes in the ownership and management of news outlets. The major networks are now owned by global conglomerates that view news not as a prestigious loss leader but as merely another profit center, no different than the NFL or *Ally McBeal*, to be milked for every possible ratings point and advertising dollar.

Changing technology also plays an important role. The news cycle has shortened: Rather than just the six o'clock evening news report we now have round-the-clock news channels like CNN, MSNBC, and Fox News, along with the Internet. Each has a voracious appetite for news to broadcast every second of every day. Inevitably, the standards for what constitutes "news" have fallen dramatically. Rumors and gossip once considered beneath the dignity of traditional journalism are now quickly disseminated, on the grounds of a common defense: "If we don't report it, someone else will—and we'll be viewed as late with the story."

We've also seen a decided politicization of ostensibly objective media outlets. Our Republican opponents have been especially skilled at driving this trend: Rush Limbaugh's radio program, GOP-TV, Pat Robertson's Christian Broadcasting Network, and many others—all seem at first glance to be objective news sources but really are propaganda operations. Again, this is not unprecedented; some newspapers and broadcasters have always reflected a strong political bias in their editorial features. But in recent years many more mainstream media have allowed their news operations to cooperate with partisan sources in producing stories that are essentially personal attacks based on negative political research.

As television has trumped print, the inherent values of a visual medium have come to dominate our understanding of events. When I was growing up, almost every home received one or more daily newspapers. Today, 70 percent of my constituents say that they get their information from television. As a result, the public's tolerance for rational, extended analysis of any issue has diminished in favor of TV's imperatives: speed, drama, and emotion rather than thought.

In recent years, the media—especially television—has been on a negative binge over government and politicians. There are countless examples; I'll just mention one. One of the major TV networks has an ongoing series of news features that spotlights examples of government waste and ineptitude ("The Fleecing of America"). The stories are often exaggerated and always one-sided, leaving viewers with the impression that government never does anything right and that virtually all of our tax dollars are wasted.

The past year has seen the apotheosis of trivialized, sensationalized coverage of politics, as entire cable networks dedicated programming to scandalous but ultimately inconsequential stories like President Clinton's affair with Monica Lewinsky. After seeing that story on TV twenty-four hours a day, seven days a week, you begin to think that rumor-mongering and character assassination is all that goes on in politics.

I don't mean to paint a bleak picture entirely. There's a positive side to some of these changes. In our wired world—where news instantly transmits to every TV and computer around the globe—war, tyranny, and crimes against humanity are more difficult to ignore or tolerate. The fall of the Berlin Wall may well have been accelerated by the ease with which the citizens of the former Soviet bloc could see, through the media, the enormous differences between the reality of life in the West and the propaganda they'd been fed by their communist rulers. The movement toward democracy all across the globe has been assisted by a vibrant, active media, the vast majority of whom work tirelessly to cover the important stories of the day.

C-SPAN, which brings the deliberations of Congress, important hearings and press conferences, and issue-oriented debates into the living rooms of millions of homes, makes a brilliant contribution to our understanding of government. But the omnipresent cameras often distort what they report. I remember Newt Gingrich, in the days before his rise to power, taking advantage of the tightly focused C-SPAN cameras to "boldly" attack the Democratic majority on television—at a time when the House chamber was nearly empty except for Gingrich and the cameraman.

Television coverage of political campaigns has done much to educate voters about the issues and positions of leading candidates. Yet the ever-dwindling attention span of the media means that the focus continues to shift away from the substance of political argument and toward the "horse race" aspects of campaigning: Who's ahead? What do the latest polls show? Which advisers are up and which are down? What are today's rumors about turmoil on the campaign trail?

Television is a tremendously powerful medium that can do so much to strengthen the bonds between citizens and their country—just as it helped one midwestern youngster, spellbound at the spectacle of a national party convention, to fall in love with politics some forty years ago. But we haven't learned to tame it. Until we do, its potential as a truly *adult* form of communication and information, one that enhances rather than undermines our status as responsible citizens, will remain unrealized.

# From Dissent to Intolerance

I t's clear that we need ways to investigate and root out wrongdoing in government. We need a competent ethics process in Congress, and we need the impeachment process as prescribed in the Constitution. (The independent counsel statute, as now written, may be another matter, however.) The danger arises when we misuse these necessary mechanisms as tools and sources for political attacks.

The dilemma of how to rigorously monitor the ethics of public officials while not allowing the mechanism to be hijacked by the politics of personal destruction is best seen in the Clinton case.

In early 1998, when we first heard stories that President Clinton had sex with a White House intern then lied about it in a deposition, I, like everyone else, was stunned. If the reports were true, I wondered, how could the president have been so irresponsible and reckless? How could someone so smart, so committed to good causes, so gifted with understanding of the real problems faced by ordinary Americans have behaved so stupidly? Like most observers, I thought that if the charges were true then President Clinton could be in real trouble, maybe even expelled from office—not necessarily by way of impeachment or other legal means but through sheer political pressure. When he publicly and emphatically denied the stories, I became reassured, and I wanted to quickly end the investigation.

But as the year went on and the damning facts gradually emerged, I was deeply disappointed and troubled by what the president had done. After his belated August confession of wrongdoing, I knew I couldn't defend what he had done. I was one of the first Democrats to describe his conduct as "reprehensible." Nonetheless, I viewed impeachment as a very different issue—as I still do.

Although I've had many occasions to work closely with Bill Clinton over the years, both before and during his presidency, we've never been social friends but rather mutually respectful political allies, and, occasionally, opponents. As Minority Leader in the House, I've never considered myself a member of the Clinton "team" but rather an independent voice among Democrats, supporting the administration whenever I could and dissenting when I felt I should. So my judgment on impeachment was no partisan knee-jerk reaction.

It was easy to decide that the president had behaved very badly. But I ultimately concluded, like many others, that what he had done did not rise to the level of an impeachable offense; it didn't seem to me to fit the category of "treason, bribery, and other high crimes and misdemeanors" specified by the Founders in our Constitution. Therefore, the most appropriate punishment for his acts was censure. Yet the Lewinsky affair, fueled by the independent counsel's costly, relentless investigation and propelled by the desire for partisan advantage on the part of some Republicans, was elevated into fodder for an impeachment debate; and once the impeachment process had begun, it quickly took on a life of its own, extremely difficult to stop or even control.

I had another, more personal reaction to the impeachment debate as well. The violent, partisan nature of the attacks on the president offended me. I had seen Bill and Hillary Clinton assaulted mercilessly before, during, and after their first campaign for the presidency in 1992. Similar attacks on their personal integrity, most without foundation, had continued unabated ever since. I don't attribute these attacks to a vast right-wing conspiracy (to use Hillary's words), but I do see a dedicated group of Clinton-haters who, for various reasons, have spent a lot of time and money attacking Clinton, trying first to prevent his election and later to overturn it. The more extreme members of this group have accused Clinton of involvement in everything from drug smuggling to murder, with no shred of evidence.

These incessant attacks against President Clinton constitute the latest, most sordid chapter in the politics of personal destruction. As we all know, violence begets violence. Unfortunately, I see no ground for optimism that we are yet ready to abandon the pattern of continuous mutual retaliation.

Another effect of this downward spiral has been the deteriorating quality of our national conversation. Political discourse in America has been getting steadily nastier, uglier, more personal, and less tolerant. Frankly, it seems as if our citizens have taken their cues from our national leaders—and what they've learned isn't good.

Twenty years ago, whenever I held a town hall meeting in my congressional district, a polite audience of citizens would attend, and we'd enjoy a vigorous but respectful debate about the issues of the day. Today, a town hall meeting usually involves a host of plac-ard-carrying demonstrators denouncing my position on some hot-button issue—gun control and abortion are two of the most heated—and the discussion is generally angry, loud, accusatory, and not very civil. When people disagree with my views or the views someone else is expressing, they scream out their disgust and disrespect. We seem to have lost the ability to disagree with others while maintaining personal respect for them.

In my experience, one of the reasons this is happening is the as-cent of the Christian Coalition as a dominant force in the Repub-lican Party. Both major parties have been dominated, from time to time, by extreme elements but never, to my knowledge, by a reli-gious group. Don't misunderstand me: There is nothing wrong with heartfelt beliefs in politics or with moral values derived from one's religion. Many of my political positions grow, ultimately, from my religious convictions. Indeed, there's a long-standing and honorable American tradition of religious involvement in politi-cal movements, from the abolition of slavery and the temperance movement to the civil rights struggles of the 1960s.

The problem comes when a group decides that its beliefs are so clearly correct that no disagreement can be tolerated. It's a short step from intolerance for another's political views to personal dis-like for that person and, ultimately, to bigotry and hatred.

I've experienced this intolerance firsthand. I'm a member of the Baptist faith, but I try to attend religious services at many different churches. A few years ago, I attended Sunday services at a church where many of the members are active supporters of the Christian Coalition. It is a large church and very active politically. In the church foyer, for example, alongside typical religious tracts you'll find stacks of Christian Coalition pamphlets featuring Pat Robertson's views. Some of the literature I saw stated, among other things, that the recently proposed Clinton budget was "anti-Christian." (It's not clear to me how we can know precisely what budget allocations Jesus would favor if he were a member of Congress.) There were also sign-up sheets for people to be picked up to vote at the next election. Religion and politics, clearly, were closely linked at this church.

On this Sunday morning, I'd brought my mother as a guest, and she and I chose seats among the congregation and settled down for the service. The minister delivered a sermon, evidently for my benefit, that made a clear political statement about controversial social issues like abortion, homosexuality, and school vouchers. The statement identified the Christian Coalition position on those issues as the only "acceptable" position.

After the service, we were surrounded by church members—not eager to say hello, to shake hands, or to welcome us to their church, but to voice their disapproval of my politics. One of the members accused me of voting in support of the "anti-Christ"—President Clinton.

I finally managed to escort my mother—a deeply religious person for all ninety years of her life—through the crowd and into our car. She turned to me and declared, "Richard, don't ever bring me back here again. These people don't follow the lessons I was taught. They are intolerant of any views but their own." I understood how she felt.

The Christian Coalition isn't a fringe group, but is the source of most of the energy in the Republican Party today. Unfortunately, the well-intentioned people who make up the vast majority of its members often don't know how their leadership has inextricably linked themselves to the political fate of the Republicans. We should condemn the politicization of their efforts without condemning their basic values and beliefs.

The growing intolerance in our society arises from dozens of sources. The radio airwaves are dotted with talk-show hosts who give angry, one-sided, often baseless presentations of their political views and scream at or cut off listeners who dare to phone with dissenting arguments. On television, *The Jerry Springer Show*— hosted by, of all things, a former midwestern mayor!—has claimed good ratings with programs featuring participants punching and mauling one another when verbal assaults seem ineffective. Even the once-sedate Sunday-morning public-affairs shows have turned into trash-talking matches, where ideologues from left and right take turns shouting at, interrupting, and insulting one another.

It all adds up to a political crisis in America—a crisis marked by growing cynicism, apathy, and anger on the part of American citizens. Nicholas Lemann, in a recent article in *The New York Times Magazine*, put it this way: "The emergence of widespread indifference, somewhat flecked with disgust, is the most distinctive phenomenon of the present day. I don't think there's ever been anything like it."

We Americans are citizen-caretakers of the longest-running continuous democracy in the history of the world. How ironic it is that we seem to be tiring of it at the very moment the rest of the world is struggling to emulate our successful experiment in freedom and self-government.

If we cannot revive our willingness to be citizens, the end result could be the loss of our citizenship and our very freedom.

If we don't stop the endless investigations and personal attacks, who will be willing to serve in public office?

If we don't restore a civil atmosphere in Congress and our state legislatures, how will we resolve our social conflicts peacefully?

If we don't reverse the growth of indifference on the part of so many citizens, how will we avoid having small minorities make our electoral decisions?

Democracy and freedom depend upon all kinds of citizen participation. Without it, they will die—maybe sooner, maybe later, but inevitably they will die.

During the 1930s, with the world in the throes of the Great Depression, educated, well-intentioned populations in Germany, Italy, Japan, and Spain turned those nations over to dictators, with catastrophic results. In the United States, we flirted with violence and totalitarianism; demagogues like Father Charles Coughlin and Huey Long enjoyed a brief vogue, and both socialist and fascist varieties of tyranny won adherents for a while. But our national roots in the democratic ideal of citizenship were too deep at that time; we renewed and redefined our political life under Franklin Roosevelt and emerged a stronger nation.

What would happen if we experienced a similar challenge today? Would we again shun the temptations of violence and dictatorship? I'm not so sure any more—that's how worried I am, and how real I think the threat is.

# Changes from the Top

The question, then, is this: How do we revive our willingness to be citizens? There are things that leaders in government can do and things that individual citizens can do.

First, we can enact genuine campaign reform that lessens the need of candidates to raise and spend enormous amounts of money.

A money spiral has been part of the cycle of violence we're living through: In every election, more and more money is poured into political campaigns, most of it being spent on increasingly negative television advertising. Restricting the amount of money spent in campaigns would have a series of beneficial consequences. There would be fewer negative ads and a greater reliance on unpaid media—traditional news outlets—in disseminating the positions of candidates. At least to a degree, the importance of image and attack in campaigning would be lessened, and the importance of a candidate's stance on the issues would be restored.

If campaigning were less costly, ordinary citizens of more modest means might be encouraged to run for public office. We're now approaching a situation where only millionaires can afford to mount a first campaign for office—a disaster for true democracy.

Reducing the need for campaign money would also reduce the influence of well-heeled special interests over policy. In time, public cynicism over the legislative decisionmaking process would be diminished. Public disdain for politicians might also be reduced by a lessening of the need for endless fund-raising; the spectacle of politicians eternally asking for money isn't calculated to increase anyone's respect for government as a calling.

For all these reasons, real campaign reform must be the highest priority of our leaders in Congress (myself included). If it takes an amendment to the U.S. Constitution to make it possible to enact campaign spending limits—on the grounds that the candidates' "free speech" would otherwise be infringed—so be it. I rarely favor tinkering with the framework our Founders devised, but I'd approve a thoughtfully crafted exception in this case.

Second, leaders in public office must actively work to put an end to the politics of personal destruction. We've seen all too clearly how violence begets violence, in a cycle that is difficult to arrest; yet violence can be stopped when enough of the participants will its end. We've seen it happen in Ireland, in Bosnia, in South Africa, and in the Middle East. It can happen here, too.

The first step is for political leaders, at all levels of government, to refuse to participate in the politics of slash and burn. It will require self-discipline, strength, and a kind of humility on all our parts: the self-discipline to forgo the advantage that might be gained through a below-the-belt attack; the strength to refuse to use an opponent's personal foibles as political weapons; the humility to admit that one's own party has no monopoly on integrity, patriotism, and compassion. There will be endless temptations to revert to the rules of the jungle; at times, they will masquerade as opportunities to land tough but fair blows on behalf of a worthy cause. We need the strength to say no even then.

If the trend starts, it may gather momentum; and if enough people in every walk of life join the trend, a critical mass can be achieved and a new, self-reinforcing, positive spiral can be started.

If our political leaders can disagree with one another while maintaining our mutual respect, the example will help all of our citizens restore civility throughout the country.

We in Congress have a special responsibility in this regard. Ours is not a parliamentary system of government like that of England, where the prime minister and the legislative majority are always, by definition, from the same party. In our system of checks and balances, the three branches of government are often controlled by different parties. It's essential, then, for partisan differences to be put aside at times for the sake of compromise; otherwise, nothing can ever be done. Thus, mutual respect and civility among the members of Congress aren't merely desirable; they are the only *practical* basis upon which our government can be run.

We owe it to the people to behave accordingly.

Third, we can change our election laws to make voting more convenient for our citizens. It should be easier to vote and easier to register to vote. People today have vastly busier and more complicated lives than in past generations, and with extended working hours and long commutes, many voters choose not to vote because of time pressures. I for one would wish that all voters would find a way, despite the difficulties, to get to their local polling place and participate; but there's no good reason why our laws and customs should make voting more difficult rather than easier.

There are several specific steps we should consider. In many countries, voting takes place on a Saturday, a Sunday, or even a national holiday, so voter participation is an easier matter. Our Constitution calls for presidential elections to be held on the first Tuesday of November; I'd support a constitutional amendment to change elections to weekend days or holidays. If that can't be passed, we should consider making every national election day a holiday, giving most people the time to vote and celebrating our democracy in the process.

It should be simple to vote no matter where you live or how recently you may have moved. In a nation where huge businesses have been built around the concept of making many of our daily activities faster and more convenient, why not apply the same know-how to voting?

Fourth, political leaders should abandon rhetoric that denounces government as the root of all evil and the cause of all problems. Of course, Republicans and conservatives are free to criticize government and to denounce specific programs with which they disagree. Exposing government inefficiency is a favor for which every citizen can be grateful.

But the unhealthy brand of antigovernment rhetoric that I take issue with is different in content and tone. It's sweeping, all-inclusive—as though *every* government program were inefficient, *all* government workers were lazy, and *no* government agency were wisely managed. Even those who indulge in this rhetoric are aware, I'm sure, that they don't really believe it. They strongly support the efforts of government in selected areas, such as national defense, air-traffic control, and crime prevention. These, somehow, are supposed to escape the otherwise general condemnation of government.

Unfortunately, the unceasing drumbeat of negativity about government doesn't really allow for intelligent distinctions. At best, it labels anyone interested in public service a fool, a phony, or a loser; at worst, it feeds the extremism of groups like the far-right militias, for whom all government is illegitimate and fair game for violent attack. We've seen where that leads. Let's agree to cool the antigovernment rhetoric and talk instead about what we can do to make government fairer, less obtrusive, more efficient, and more responsive—not pretend we can wish it away.

## From the Grass Roots

Obviously, actions by public officials alone will not solve this crisis. Citizens must take action as well if our crisis of faith in democracy is to be resolved.

First, we must all take the simplest, most basic step toward full citizenship by voting in every election for which we're eligible. In the 1996 presidential election, fewer than 50 percent of registered voters cast a ballot—and that figure, of course, doesn't take into account the millions who aren't registered. The turnout in local and primary elections is much worse. In August 1998, we held a primary election in Missouri for which only 15 percent of those registered turned out. Frankly, I think it's a disgrace—especially when compared with the 70–80 percent turnouts we see in some of the emerging democracies of Central and South America.

We need to consciously change our social attitude toward not voting, just as we've consciously changed our attitudes toward drunken driving and sexual harassment, heaping well-deserved scorn upon activities we once winked at or ignored. Voting should be recognized as the civic duty of every adult citizen, not an optional exercise for those with some special interest in politics.

We can start by dispelling the myth that one vote "doesn't count." Your one vote, in the right circumstances, may be absolutely crucial. Many school bond issues have been won or lost in my congressional district by fewer than fifty votes; many elections for Congress are won or lost by fewer than a hundred votes. You can never know what kind of difference the vote you *didn't* cast might have made.

Or think of voting as a matter of sheer self-interest. When the majority of citizens fail to vote, they allow a minority to make decisions that affect all of us. It baffles me how a nation of people that rose up in outrage over the prospect of not being able to choose their own family doctors can willingly put up with that.

Furthermore, that voting minority may be—increasingly *is*—a well-organized group with a special agenda directly opposed to the interests of the majority. I think particularly here of the power of the National Rifle Association, which has opposed gun-control measures like a mandatory waiting period before buying a handgun so police records can be checked. Such rules are supported by an overwhelming number of Americans, but the single-interest voting behavior of the minority of people who oppose them makes them almost impossible to enact.

The old saying goes, "If you don't vote, you can't gripe." To that I'd add, "If you don't vote, you may eventually lose the *right* to vote." Democracy depends on participation, and without active citizens reenergizing democracy it is no given that democracy will last.

Second, citizens should get involved working for the campaigns of candidates they like. Especially on the local level, you'd be amazed at the power even a handful of willing volunteers can wield. I've been telling everyone I know about Jan Schakowsky, a candidate for Congress in 1998 who took on the Chicago political machine and won against all odds. Her secret weapon? An ad in *Roll Call*, a national political newspaper, asking for volunteer campaign workers. Jan offered a unique deal: Anyone willing to pay for their own transportation to Chicago and work in her campaign for four or five weeks would be treated to an intensive, two-week "school of politics," in which they'd learn organizing and management skills they could apply to campaigns in their home districts or anywhere else. More than seventy volunteers came to Chicago from all over the country, taking leaves of absence from responsible jobs and busy lives to learn and participate in the political process. They bunked in the homes and apartments of Jan's supporters, who also fixed them home-cooked meals. This team of irregulars won a stunning electoral victory for Jan's campaign, reigniting their own faith in democracy in the process.

Veteran Chicago precinct captains told Jan that they'd never seen such talented political workers. And I'm so excited about her plan that I'm hoping to have her conduct seminars for all our Democratic congressional candidates in 2000, so they can steal a bit of her genius.

Don't let anyone tell you that you can't jump into politics as a novice and make a difference—immediately. The experience shared by all of Jan's volunteers proves you can.

Third, citizens should volunteer to run for office or take on a cause to help improve the community. Virtually every problem you've ever complained about can be matched to a solution any concerned citizen can pursue. Worried about the quality of your kids' schooling? Run for a seat on the local school board and help change the policies that hamstring creative teachers. Unhappy with the way a local factory is encroaching on precious parkland? Run for town council or the local zoning board and play a role in setting and enforcing tough land-use standards.

Running for office isn't the only approach, of course. A determined activist armed with little more than a telephone, a home computer, and a little gumption can work near-miracles. Recent

history is full of examples of individual citizens like the courageous crusader Lois Gibbs who took on polluters and forced the
clean up of New York's Love Canal or the mothers who founded
Mothers Against Drunk Driving, the group that has done so much
to combat drunken driving. They raised their voices, made themselves heard, and made their communities better places for all.

Dissidents in China, imprisoned for merely stating their political views, are fighting a lifelong battle to enjoy the freedoms that
most Americans take for granted. The least we can do is to make
good use of the freedoms we enjoy.

Fourth, citizens should let their representatives at all levels of
government know their views on issues. As a congressman, I get a
lot of letters, phone calls, and email, and I consider it all when
making policy decisions. If you really want to make an impact, request a personal interview; many representatives have open office
hours or town hall meetings that you can attend for face-to-face
conversation. Don't keep your opinions to yourself—we in government need the guidance and counsel only caring citizens can
offer.

Fifth, join local organizations of every kind—community
clubs, professional associations, labor committees, interfaith
groups, fraternal organizations, what have you—and work to make
them vital, involved members of the community. This doesn't
necessarily mean supporting political candidates. It does mean
making your voices heard on issues you're concerned or knowledgeable about, and it means donating your group's time, talent,
and treasure in support of worthy causes to preserve and
strengthen our social fabric.

A century and a half ago, French visitor Alexis de Tocqueville
remarked that one of the great strengths of American democracy

was the tendency of the people to form, join, and support voluntary organizations of a hundred kinds. That's still true today. Such groups not only do a lot of important and beneficial work in their communities but also produce citizens with a habit of involvement and a talent for leadership. We need such citizens more today than ever before.

So much good work is possible for citizens who really take ownership of their communities; so much is already being done. Let me tell you about an example from my beloved St. Louis.

They call my hometown the "Gateway to the West," in commemoration of the crucial role St. Louis played in the exploration and settling of America, with the completion of the Louisiana Purchase in 1804. One hundred years after that historic event, which nearly doubled the size of the youthful United States, St. Louis celebrated in exuberant style with the 1904 World's Fair (at which, among other things, the ice-cream cone was invented).

About a decade ago, many of us noticed that the Louisiana Purchase *bi*centennial was fast approaching. Since we Missourians love celebrating, citizens' groups began meeting to discuss how we ought to mark the occasion when the year 2004 rolled around.

The first and most obvious idea was to host another World's Fair. But the more people met and talked, the more they felt that a "party," however grand, wasn't what the city needed most. Instead, they thought, why not use the occasion to address the many long-range problems faced by St. Louis—like so many other American cities?

Thousands of citizens and dozens of civic groups have come together around this idea. Already, a host of efforts are under way, to culminate in 2004, to renovate, restore, improve, and revitalize the region—from its educational system and its health care facilities to its roads and bridges, parks, museums, and historic sites.

I'm proud that my hometown is setting such a wonderful example of how citizen participation can change the life of an entire community for the better. And if you care to visit St. Louis in 2004, please do. We won't be having a World's Fair, but we'll have lots to show off, I promise.

## Failure Is Not an Option

You probably saw the movie *Apollo 13*, starring that likeable middle-American actor Tom Hanks, our generation's answer to Jimmy Stewart. It tells the true-life story of a moon mission saved from fatal disaster only by the courage, quick-wittedness, and tenacity of the spacecraft's crew and their support team on earth.

One turning point in the movie occurs when the mission's project director orders his staff to construct a replacement air filter from a collection of spare parts, tape, wire, and other junk available inside the spacecraft. It sounds like a joke, but it's deadly serious; in fact, without a new filter, the astronauts will surely die. "Failure," the director solemnly intones, "is not an option." Sure enough, the team succeeds—and Tom Hanks and the rest of the crew are saved.

We've reached a turning point in our nation's history. Yet the crisis we face is a deceptive one. There's no external enemy poised to invade our shores; neither economic collapse nor civil war threatens us from within. But we've allowed a variety of causes to gradually erode some of the most vital underpinnings of our democratic system.

We never meant it to happen. At times, we were distracted by other concerns—the turmoil of Vietnam, the struggle for racial justice, the endgame of the Cold War, the ideological battles of the "culture wars." Yet, little by little, our faith in free institutions freely elected; our willingness to settle disputes peaceably through civil discourse; our respect for the humanity, integrity, and patriotism of our political opponents—all these were whittled away. What's left is a hollow core of what citizenship was meant to be—a frail structure, all too likely to topple in the next fierce wind.

We Americans face a variety of challenges as we enter the next century. That's always been the case. I've spoken to some of them in this book: global business competition; the quiet crisis of inadequate time for families; the erosion of living standards and retirement security; the need to reform and revitalize our health care and educational systems. They're all important, and they'll be the subject of intense debate in the months and years to come, as they should be.

But I hope that the overarching problem of the decline of faith in democracy—the larger context within which we'll tackle all the issues we face—isn't overlooked. If we ignore the decay of citizenship, I'm afraid that its consequences will make it far more difficult for us to solve our economic, social, and other problems. By contrast, if we successfully meet the challenge of revitalizing and renewing our concept of citizenship—if we find ways to empower more and more of our citizens to take true ownership of our government institutions, our community resources, and our nation's future course—I'm sure there's no problem we can't solve.

Can we make the America of the twenty-first century the "even better place" that the title of this book foreshadows? There's no doubt we can. It remains to be seen whether we Americans—all of us—possess the inner strength to do so. For us, as for the crew of *Apollo 13*—gallant voyagers of uncertain prospects but tenacious will—failure is not an option.

CONCLUSION

# The Mission Ahead

February 4, 1999, was a noteworthy day for me. In a short speech before the House Democratic Caucus, I announced that I would not run for president in the year 2000. Instead, I decided to set my sights once again on representing Missouri's Third Congressional District in the United States Congress. I'll also work hard on behalf of Democratic candidates all around the country in hopes that our party can reclaim control of the House of Representatives. If we succeed, I hope to become the Speaker of the House—the job once held by the great Democratic leader Tip O'Neill, a position I'd be deeply honored to occupy.

As the start of the 2000 election campaign approached, I'd spent several months weighing this decision. The choice wasn't obvious at first. There's no more powerful or prestigious job in the world than that of president of the United States, and I'd be lying if I said that I didn't tingle just a bit at the thought of being elected to that office by our nation's citizens. In that sense, I'm no different from any other politician. And many of my closest supporters had urged me to consider running. No other likely candidate offers quite the same combination of experience and policy views that I offer, and some of those I've worked with closely over the years would have liked to see me carry a presidential campaign banner on behalf of the causes we share.

In the end, however, my decision came down to one key question: Where could I make the greatest contribution toward furthering the goals I believe in? As this book has explained, I feel strongly about the kinds of social, economic, and political changes our nation needs to make in order to cope with the dislocations and challenges of the new global marketplace. I intend to speak out about these issues no matter what my position. But in which role could my voice have the greatest and most useful impact?

After much soul-searching, prayer, and honest conversation with the people closest to me—family, friends, colleagues, supporters—I came to one clear conclusion: I'm a very lucky person to have been given the job of representing the people of St. Louis in the United States Congress, still the greatest legislative body in the history of the world. It's a job I think I've gotten pretty good at, one that I'd like to keep.

I originally got into public life out of a desire to try to improve the lives of the people of Missouri's Third Congressional District. That remains my focus. In helping them, I think, I can help all the people who are proud of America—of our tolerance, our commitment to freedom, our dedication to our homes and communities.

What about my desire to return control of the House of Representatives to the Democratic Party? I think it's an important goal, and not just in terms of political one-upmanship. I always recall a favorite adage of mine—"Elections have consequences." It *matters* to our people who controls the agenda in Congress and who holds the balance of power when legislation that can help or hinder our nation's progress is on the line.

I'm as competitive as the next person; everyone in politics is, I'm sure. But the battle for control of the next Congress isn't just about perks or prestige—who chairs a committee or wields the gavel on the House floor. More important, it's about helping the millions of parents who have less time to spend with their children amid the increasing demands of work, it's about making sure our nation guarantees all our people the skills they need to compete in the new economy, it's about protecting our retirement security and making health care available to all—in fact, it's about the entire range of policy choices we'll be facing that affects every American.

It's also about the way we do business in the House of Representatives. As I've described in these pages, Congress has largely lost the trust of the American people. It has allowed the politics of personal destruction, not the politics of progress, to rule the day. It has driven members of different parties apart and has seemingly closed the book on a time when members could really work together, despite partisan differences, on behalf of the people.

All that must change. We need a United States Congress that reflects the hopes and the dreams of the people rather than the unending drumbeat of a small minority bent on imposing its will upon an entire nation. We need a more civil, tolerant, openhearted House in which the *people's* good becomes the first and final objective.

Politics is often seen as a zero-sum game, and in some ways it is. When one party claims control of an office or wins a majority of seats in a legislative body, the other party loses. It's a winners take-all system that inevitably produces intense partisan feelings.

I wouldn't change the system that our nation's Founders laid out in the Constitution even if I could. But I believe we can restore civility to the competition and make it more a battle of ideas than a clash of personalities. Such a return to nobler visions of politics and of citizenship is vital to our nation's future and, indeed, the world's.

Right now, I think returning the Democrats to the majority in Congress would best return us to a politics of values and ideals. I don't think that either political party has a corner on virtue. But I feel now the Democrats in Congress have been speaking best to people's everyday concerns and highest ideals. If we win, and I'm elected Speaker of the House, I hope to lead the House to a return to civility. Some Democratic Members may want to exact revenge if we win. We cannot follow that course if we want to return to the politics of ideals.

I think we've reached a critical moment in the history of our political system and specifically of Congress. The next several years will see a battle for the soul of the institution, a struggle to determine whether it will sink further into the morass of slash-and-burn politics or turn back to the better ways of an earlier time. I want to be around to help lead the battle.

We live during a time when Americans everywhere need to re-focus their energies not on power, personal ambition, and mone-tary gain but on the national good. It would be harder for me to spread this message if I were simultaneously promoting myself for higher office. America needs more citizens who will devote them-selves to preserving, improving, reforming, and nurturing the places in which they find themselves today—their families, their communities, their schools, their workplaces. That's an effort to which I want to contribute in the years to come, not just by words but by example.

Shortly after the fall of the Berlin Wall in 1989, I had the oppor-tunity to travel to Eastern Europe to visit the countries that had

until recently been dominated by the Soviet Union. I was awed by the enthusiasm of people everywhere for the opportunities that now lay before them, unshackled from the yokes of communist totalitarianism. The economies of these countries were in disarray (and still face enormous difficulties today); the skies, streams, and landscapes were fouled by decades of uncontrolled pollution; the educational and health systems were rigid and antiquated. *But at last the people were free.* This made all the difference—and they knew it.

In Prague, Czechoslovakia, I visited with a group of youthful democracy activists known as the Civic Forum. They were the idealists who had helped foster change under the old regime and brokered the transition to the new, self-governing Czechoslovakia (later the Czech Republic). They were led by Vaclav Havel, the much-admired playwright and essayist, who'd spent four and a half years in prison for his human rights activism and who would later be elected the first president of the new nation.

At our meeting, in the basement of a Prague beer hall, I presented the leaders with a copy of the Bill of Rights, the original ten amendments to the U.S. Constitution. Tears in their eyes, they told me how the ideals embodied in the Bill of Rights had inspired them during their years of underground struggle on behalf of basic human freedom. And they told me that, to them, the familiar image of the majestic dome atop the U.S. Capitol, and the Congress it housed, were undying symbols of freedom and democracy.

I was flooded with emotions of my own. Yes, I felt pride that these courageous young men and women looked to America for inspiration. But I felt more than a little anger, too. I was angry that America—at the very moment when the ideas for which this country had long stood were winning over the world—might very well be losing the will to secure and consolidate such a glorious victory.

Years later, I met Wei Jingsheng, a leader of the democracy movement in China. I've spoken of him elsewhere in these pages. Released from prison on "medical parole" by the Chinese leadership, he took up exile here in America. Shortly after his release, he visited with me and with Congresswoman Nancy Pelosi, herself a true hero in the fight for democracy and freedom in China. Wei thanked us for our voices, saying that they'd helped give hope to him and to thousands of others unfairly imprisoned in China simply for advocating internationally recognized human rights. For Wei, as for the Polish freedom fighters and for their counterparts the world over, Congress was a symbol, a beacon.

These people and millions of others all around the globe have looked to the United States for leadership—not because of our military or economic might but because of our commitment to democracy. If we're to maintain that leadership, we must revitalize the ideal of citizenship here at home, bring new integrity to our political processes, and return civility and tolerance to our public discourse.

Each of us, in different ways, can make a difference—to our children, to our communities, to our nation. But doing so will require a new sense of purpose, a renewal of activism and citizenship, and an understanding that we're all in this together.

It's a mission to which we must devote ourselves. It's a mission dedicated to America's future and to the future of all humankind—one worthy of the lives of free men and women. I hope you'll join me in it.

# ACKNOWLEDGMENTS

I started talking about writing a book shortly after I withdrew from the presidential race in 1988. I believed that if people had better understood what I had to say, I'd have had more success in that race. Unfortunately, election campaigns in today's world are usually more about sound bites than they are about complex programs and thoughtful analysis. A book, I thought, might give me the opportunity to convey my ideas more fully.

But during the ensuing years I came to realize that I didn't want to write just another book by a politician—a campaign book filled with rhetoric and prepackaged reflections. Such a book would have done more for me than for the reader. Instead, I decided to write a book that's both a self-help guide to the new economy and a message of concern—and ultimately optimism—about the state of citizen involvement in American democracy. It's a call to arms and to action.

Since becoming a member of Congress, I've had the opportunity to travel the country and the world, observing and learning. What I've found is that fundamental change isn't usually the result of some program designed in Washington, D.C., but rather is the result of average people—citizens—taking control of their own destinies and making a difference. Government plays an important role, but in the end it's all about people—average, everyday people making a real difference in their lives and the lives of their communities. I hope this book has accurately reflected that discovery.

There are too many people I'd like to thank to list them all here. But as most of the winners on Oscar night say, there are some people I can't refrain from mentioning.

First, there are the people who've taken the time to share their stories with me. I've met hundreds of them, in factories and offices, schools and living rooms, and they've been more generous with their time and energy than I could have dreamed. Not all of their stories are retold in this book, but I hope that they all understand how thankful I am for their kindness.

Second, I want to thank my staff who have so ably helped me over the years. They've worked long hours and made enormous sacrifices, usually without fanfare or special recognition, and I'd be lost without them. They are public servants in the highest sense of the term.

Third, I want to single out Jeff Faux and the Economic Policy Institute for their help in understanding some of the basic changes affecting people in today's economy. Jeff and his staff work tirelessly as advocates for a progressive agenda promoting a high and rising standard of living for all Americans.

I also must mention Barry Bluestone, the eternal optimist about what people can achieve if given a chance; the leaders of organized labor who have stood by my side over the years and who fight for their members every day, refusing to compromise their basic values; and David Kusnet, for helping to get this project out of the starting blocks as well as for his steadfast belief in progressive politics. There are many, many others.

I want to thank publisher Peter Osnos for believing in this project. Peter and I first met at National Airport in Washington, D.C., one afternoon, and within thirty minutes I knew that I wanted PublicAffairs to publish this book. Books are commercial products, and every publisher wants them to sell. But Peter always supported this work as more than just another product, encouraging me to write the book that I truly wanted to write. His advice and counsel over the months have been deeply appreciated.

I also want to thank Geoff Shandler, my editor at PublicAffairs, who helped guide the project through. At times, we wondered whether we'd ever really get the book done, but Geoff's faith never wavered. And my thanks to editorial consultant Karl Weber, who joined us for the homestretch. His insights and understanding helped me immeasurably.

As the world enters a new millennium, this book presents part of a living agenda for change—that continual process of growth, learning, and experimentation in which we all share. And of all the human experiments in culture, science, technology, and economics that are flourishing around the world today, none is so vital and promising as the experiment in self-governance we call democracy. I hope this book, in some small measure, may help to keep it alive.

# INDEX

# Index

# Index

# Index

# Index

# Index

PUBLICAFFAIRS is a new nonfiction publishing house and a tribute to the standards, values, and flair of three persons who have served as mentors to countless reporters, writers, editors, and book people of all kinds, including me.

I. F. STONE, proprietor of *I. F. Stone's Weekly*, combined a commitment to the First Amendment with entrepreneurial zeal and reporting skill and became one of the great independent journalists in American history. At the age of eighty, Izzy published *The Trial of Socrates*, which was a national bestseller. He wrote the book after he taught himself ancient Greek.

BENJAMIN C. BRADLEE was for nearly thirty years the charismatic editorial leader of *The Washington Post*. It was Ben who gave the *Post* the range and courage to pursue such historic issues as Watergate. He supported his reporters with a tenacity that made them fearless, and it is no accident that so many became authors of influential, best-selling books.

ROBERT L. BERNSTEIN, the chief executive of Random House for more than a quarter century, guided one of the nation's premier publishing houses. Bob was personally responsible for many books of political dissent and argument that challenged tyranny around the globe. He is also the founder and was the longtime chair of Human Rights Watch, one of the most respected human rights organizations in the world.

. . .

For fifty years, the banner of Public Affairs Press was carried by its owner Morris B. Schnapper, who published Gandhi, Nasser, Toynbee, Truman, and about 1,500 other authors. In 1983 Schnapper was described by *The Washington Post* as "a redoubtable gadfly." His legacy will endure in the books to come.

Peter Osnos, *Publisher*